Breath of Gold

Created by

Adrienne Rivera and contributing authors: Susan Peters, Shawn LaFountain, Tracey-Ann Rose, Erin Kathleen Cummings, Rachel Gossett, Terese Katz, Kara Stoltenberg, Simona Luna, Amy Quinn and Veronica Galipo.

Foreword by Jeremy Youst

Published by Adrienne Rivera, LLC

https://www.breathofgold.com/

ISBN: 9798305318906

Cover design by The Soulshine Creative

Interior design by Muhammad Imran

Printed in USA

First Edition

Library of Congress Cataloging-in-Publication Data [Include if applicable - usually provided by the Library of Congress]

Disclaimer: This book is intended for informational purposes only and is not a substitute for therapy or professional medical advice; please consult your doctor before trying breathwork.

Circular connected breath is not recommended for people with the following conditions: pregnancy, schizophrenia, bipolar disorder, any major heart condition (including past history of heart attack), any major neurological condition (including stroke, epilepsy, seizures, or recent head injury), history of aneurysms (personal or family), recent surgeries, serious eye issues (such as glaucoma or retinal detachment), active addiction or substance use, or any other serious health condition for which you are under a doctor's care.

Dedication

This book is dedicated to my abuela and abuelo (my Puerto Rican grandparents).

Thank you for being such strong spiritual teachers in my life. Thank you for showing me the infinite capacity of love and how much love our hearts can truly hold.

Abuela, thank you for showing me your love through every little thing you've done.

I'll never forget when you gave me a little pillow with the words "Te Amo," (I love you) on it.

It was the way that you gave it to me that made it so special. You said, "Mi amor, eso es un pedacito de mi corazón. Siempre estaré contigo." (My love, I give you a piece of my heart. I will always be with you.)

My abuela showed me how to truly give love to others. She gave me an infinite abundance of love. She made me feel good enough (even though my Spanish wasn't perfect).

She made me feel loved unconditionally, without even knowing any of my accomplishments.

And Abuelo, your joy and your infectious heart has opened my heart so fully. The way that you would always smile and be so excited to see us when we would visit makes me so happy.

The depth of your spiritual connection was the first experience I ever had with feeling how deep a human could really be.

Your love and appreciation for music was so spiritually moving. I feel that same connection to the power of music and spirituality as well.

I know that both of you are so proud of me doing this deep spiritual work with breathwork. I know you with always be with me forever.

I love you always.

Foreword

Written by Jeremy Youst, Founder of Power of Breath Institute

Some people may consider me to be one of the "grandfather's" of modern day breathwork. As a trained psychotherapist with over 30 years of experience practicing Somatic Breath Therapy—my own approach to therapeutic breathwork—I've dedicated my career to harnessing the healing power of breath.

If you've never experienced breathwork, now might be the perfect time to explore it. There are many skilled practitioners and schools listed on the GPBA and IBF websites, including the cutting-edge Breath of Gold training.

I first met Adrienne Rivera, founder of Breath of Gold, when she invited me to be a guest teacher at the Breath of Gold Festival. From the moment we met, I was struck by her vibrant energy and unwavering passion for breathwork and its potential to transform lives. It was a pleasure to contribute my years of knowledge to such an inspiring space.

My journey into breathwork began in the late 1980s with a transformative Rebirthing breathwork session. These early experiences opened my eyes to the profound effects of harnessing high states of prana, enabling me to unlock and integrate deep-seated beliefs related to childhood trauma. This foundational insight propelled me into further training in Transformational Breath and ultimately led to the establishment of the Power of Breath Institute and the development of Somatic Breath Therapy.

In 1989, I attended a breathwork retreat in Key Largo, FL, where I encountered a life-changing event. During a session, an intense rush of energy surged through me, and I experienced a state of transcendence that felt like entering "The White Room of God." In that moment, I was enveloped in light, peace, and a profound sense of connection. This extraordinary experience not only demonstrated the transformative power of breath but also ignited my lifelong passion for this healing practice.

A second transformative experience occurred during another retreat, where I floated in the ocean and felt a profound connection to the vastness of the Earth and the cosmos.

In that moment, I dissolved all boundaries and became one with the universe. These powerful experiences reinforced my commitment to breathwork as my soul's calling.

In 2001, I co-founded the Power of Breath Institute in southern New Hampshire, where I dedicated 22 years to a full-time breathwork practice, conducting over 8,000 sessions and leading practitioner training in both New Hampshire and Ireland. I've had the privilege of teaching at esteemed venues like the Omega Institute and the Psychotherapy Symposium in Washington, D.C., and I served as the USA National Coordinator for the International Breathwork Federation (IBF).

To deepen my trauma-informed approach, I've had the privilege of studying with leading experts such as Dr. Dan Siegel, Dr. Bessel van der Kolk, and Dr. Stephen Porges. My 18 years as a board member of the Global Professional Breathwork Alliance (GPBA) also allowed me to contribute to the revision of international breathwork training standards.

Becoming a professional breathwork practitioner is a lifelong journey, where your own breathwork journeys are often your best teachers. While many excellent trainers exist, true mastery of breathwork transcends online courses and videos. It requires personal practice and a profound understanding of techniques to deliver meaningful, integrity-driven sessions. Engaging in a comprehensive program like Breath of Gold is essential for building competency and upholding high standards within the field of therapeutic breathwork.

Getting to know Adrienne has revealed her to be an incredible breathwork teacher—clear, attentive, insightful, and smart. She excels in conveying the principles I emphasize in my breathwork facilitator programs, particularly the A.R.T. (Awareness, Relationality, Technique) of therapeutic breathwork.

In assisting her with some of her training topics, I have found her to teach attentively and beautifully with students through well-defined and vibrant teachings, answering questions with sensitivity and depth. I have found her to be skilled at facilitating breathwork online with groups, which is an artform in itself.

Circular Connected Breath, often referred to as conscious connected breathwork or therapeutic breathwork, is a transformative body-based modality known for its efficacy in healing anxiety, depression, trauma, PTSD, and emotional dysregulation. This approach harnesses the power of conscious breathing to facilitate shifts in mental and emotional states.

This style is the primary method I employ with my clients, and it's also the core practice that Adrienne guides her clients through at Breath of Gold. For millennia, cultures around the world have utilized conscious breathing to attain altered states of consciousness, inner peace, and spiritual connection. In contemporary times, pioneers such as Ilse Middendorf, Wilhelm Reich, Stanislav Grof (known for Holotropic Breathwork), and Leonard Orr (Rebirthing) have integrated breathwork into modern therapeutic practices, using it to address trauma and enhance physical, mental, and emotional well-being.

Conscious connected breathing involves intentional, circular breath patterns that cultivate body awareness, alleviate stress, enhance mental clarity, and promote spiritual connection. It provides a pathway for healing trauma and PTSD by enabling individuals to revisit subconscious memories and release stored emotional energy.

Therapeutic breathwork works by removing pauses between breaths, creating a continuous, circular flow that amplifies prana, or life energy. This process empowers participants to actively engage in their healing journey, making it both a somatic and cognitive experience.

In assisting her with some of her training topics, I have found her to teach attentively and beautifully with students through well-defined and vibrant teachings, answering questions with sensitivity and depth. I have found her to be skilled at facilitating breathwork online with groups, which is an artform in itself.

Circular Connected Breath, often referred to as conscious connected breathwork or therapeutic breathwork, is a transformative body-based modality known for its efficacy in healing anxiety, depression, trauma, PTSD, and emotional dysregulation. This approach harnesses the power of conscious breathing to facilitate shifts in mental and emotional states.

This style is the primary method I employ with my clients, and it's also the core practice that Adrienne guides her clients through at Breath of Gold. For millennia, cultures around the world have utilized conscious breathing to attain altered states of consciousness, inner peace, and spiritual connection. In contemporary times, pioneers such as Ilse Middendorf, Wilhelm Reich, Stanislav Grof (known for Holotropic Breathwork), and Leonard Orr (Rebirthing) have integrated breathwork into modern therapeutic practices, using it to address trauma and enhance physical, mental, and emotional well-being.

Conscious connected breathing involves intentional, circular breath patterns that cultivate body awareness, alleviate stress, enhance mental clarity, and promote spiritual connection. It provides a pathway for healing trauma and PTSD by enabling individuals to revisit subconscious memories and release stored emotional energy.

Therapeutic breathwork works by removing pauses between breaths, creating a continuous, circular flow that amplifies prana, or life energy. This process empowers participants to actively engage in their healing journey, making it both a somatic and cognitive experience.

I am excited to see that Adrienne Rivera is sharing the magic of breathwork all around the world. I am honored to be a guest teacher in the Breath of Gold Breathwork Facilitator Program and to have experienced Adrienne's breathwork journeys myself.
In this book, you'll get to hear about some of the life-changing breathwork experiences that her clients and students have had.

I hope that this book inspires you to fully harness the power of your breath.

Breath of Gold
Table of Contents

Introduction

Written by Adrienne Rivera, Founder of Breath of Gold

Tears filled my eyes as a wave of pleasure and euphoria overcame every cell in my body. I had never experienced such physical pleasure. The message was clear: "Everything you need lies within your breath."

It was a revelation. Everything I sought was already within me. Before that first breathwork journey, I'd searched for fulfillment outside myself, turning to food for comfort, shopping for a sense of worth, and relationships to fill a void. But in that transformative breathwork experience, I felt a surge of empowerment that I had never experienced before.

The realization that this power resided within me, accessible at any time through my breath, was exhilarating. I couldn't believe something as simple as breathwork could move me so deeply, to the point of tears. An overwhelming amount of energy coursed through my body, more than I ever imagined possible.

As humans, we often seek fulfillment externally. Breathwork has taught me that everything we need resides within. I've learned far more from breathwork than from any book or spiritual teacher. My hope is that this book inspires you to cultivate a relationship with yourself through breathwork, or to deepen your existing practice. You'll be moved by the stories of those who have transformed their lives through their experiences with Breath of Gold.

My First Breathwork Experiences

My first breathwork journey revealed to me that "everything I was looking for lies within my breath." The next few breathwork journeys were wildly different. In one session, I felt an old ankle injury pulsating with pain. The message I received was clear: new life force energy was here to heal the stagnant energy. For over a decade, I'd experienced a dull ache in my ankle from that injury. Since that session, the pain has vanished. I run pain-free now, likely due to the healing that occurred during that breathwork experience.

Another early journey taught me how to grieve. As humans, we often lack the tools and guidance to navigate grief. Yet, loss is inevitable. If we can't process those feelings, we can't move through the pain and truly heal.

My first significant experience with grief was the unexpected loss of my friend, Dan, who died from a rattlesnake bite. When he passed, I resisted feeling the love and grief in my heart. I found myself bargaining with myself, trying to rationalize why I shouldn't feel sad.

"We weren't that close," I thought. *"You didn't know him that long."*

It felt easier to avoid the pain.

Instead of processing my grief, I tried to move on quickly, believing I could bypass the sadness. 'I'll just stay busy,' I told myself, 'and eventually, I'll forget about it.' That's what I did —I distracted myself—instead of allowing myself to grieve. I put my head down, worked hard, and avoided my feelings.

Three days after learning about Dan's passing, I attended an in-person group breathwork session. Tears flowed throughout the entire ninety minutes. Afterward, the facilitator asked what I was releasing. She shared that she could feel my emotions moving powerfully through my tears, yet sensed I wasn't in pain. I told her I was honoring Dan, feeling the kindness of his heart, and appreciating his positive impact on my life. I remember her saying, "Wow, that's what grief looks like. *That's what tears of grief look like.*"

It was profoundly healing. Opening my heart to these feelings through breathwork transformed how I approach love and loss.

My First Breathwork Retreat

My first ten breathwork experiences were life-changing. I'll always remember my first breathwork retreat. I manifested an opportunity to attend a river rafting breathwork retreat led by the very people who introduced me to this practice. I was immediately excited and knew I was meant to be there.

While carpooling to the Green River with other participants, we shared our intentions for the retreat. Setting intentions is a powerful way to enhance a breathwork experience by bringing to light what needs healing. My turn was approaching, and I searched for my answer. Gazing at the blur of passing pine trees, I asked myself, "What is my intention? What am I ready to heal?" The message arrived with a visceral force in my gut: "You've been guided here to release fear." *"Fear of what?"* I wondered. "Fear of everything."

I carried so much fear in my body: fear of success, fear of failure, fear of being alone, fear of dying, fear of not being safe, fear of venturing outside my comfort zone, fear of bugs and spiders, fear of the dark—you name it, I feared it.

"Am I truly ready to release all of these fears?" I wondered.

The answer resonated with certainty: *"Yes. You are ready."*

I knew I could release my fears, and I committed to that intention for the retreat.

As it turns out, I manifested the perfect opportunity to confront my fears! After hours of rafting down the Green River, we arrived at the campsite I'd be sharing with twenty other participants. To my surprise, the entire campsite was infested with ants! *"How am I going to do this?"* I panicked. *"How can I possibly surrender to this for the next four days?"*

Growing up in the suburbs of Washington, D.C., with minimal exposure to nature, I felt completely out of my comfort zone.

For the first ten minutes, I practically did high knees, hiding behind a tree in tears, terrified of ants crawling up my legs and into my sleeping bag.

With not much choice, I began to surrender. I sat at a picnic table, ready for dinner. As the sun set, the ants disappeared from sight, and my fear subsided. I found myself comfortably placing my feet flat on the earth.

The next day, I felt slightly braver, no longer needing high socks or swatting imaginary ants every five seconds. I surrendered even more when I laid down on the forest floor for breathwork. Of course, the ants were still there, crawling between my toes and over my feet. But something inside me was shifting. I smiled. The message I heard within was clear: *"The ants are your angels."* I understood I needn't be afraid. They were my little healing helpers.

With each breathwork session at the retreat, I processed past traumas and deepened my connection with my inner child. I felt more connected to myself and present than ever before.

Later, we participated in a cacao ceremony led by Aja and Danny, the retreat leaders. They instructed us to hold a warm mug of cacao against our hearts, gaze into it, and speak our intentions into the brew. Until that moment, I had never been so intentional with food. This practice sparked a profound awareness within me, releasing powerful emotions. Tears streamed down my face as memories from the past six years of battling binge eating disorder surfaced. I put on my sunglasses to hide my tears, recalling moments when I felt completely out of control with food—times when I'd come home and eat in secret, searching for comfort and love. Those were tears of sadness, awareness, and self-acceptance.

After the cacao ceremony, we participated in a water healing ceremony in the river beside our campsite. Twenty of us formed a circle, each taking turns entering the center. I watched as others led by releasing emotions through screams, then moving intuitively, following their inner guidance. When ready, they plunged into the water, turning onto their backs to float, arms and legs outstretched. One by one, we placed our hands on the person in the water, sending healing energy.

Finally, it was my turn. Standing in the center, I noticed my fear of cold water surface, along with other fears I still held within. I screamed with all my might, then chose to faceplant into the water, slowly rolling onto my back to float. Each person's hand gently landed on my body, one by one, the last resting on my belly.

Throughout my entire life up until that point, it had felt like my belly was upside down and in a knot. As soon as the last person placed their hand on my belly, I experienced my first somatic release.

I did not expect this to be so life-changing for me. I started hyperventilating, the tears flowing and my breath becoming uncontrollable. It was incredibly healing. No one tried to diminish my experience, tell me it was too much, or stop what was happening. They simply witnessed and held space for my emotions to be felt and released.

In my mind's eye, I saw a portal of golden light open from that person's hand, releasing all the physical pain and tightness from my belly. My solar plexus released the tightness, and I visualized it rising and dissolving into the sky. That physical tightness in my stomach hasn't returned since that water healing ceremony. The experience showed me that unresolved traumas are trapped inside our bodies and must be processed and released.

Afterward, we did a breathwork session. I received a clear message: *"fix your mommy issues."* *"Well, that's weird,"* I thought. *"I thought my mom and I were cool."* Then I remembered a story she once told me: When I was less than a year old, my sister was crying downstairs, and my mother, thinking it was an emergency, rushed down, accidentally dropping me. That's how I broke my leg as a baby.

In that moment I thought to myself: *"I bet you that's where all of the fear has been steming from–from early developmental years."* I went from feeling safe, held, and loved, pressed against my mother's bosom, to being abruptly dropped and injured. It made sense that my subconscious learned to distrust the world, to expect safety to vanish in an instant. As I breathed deeply through that session, I connected with that past version of myself and released the fear. *"I healed just fine,"* I reassured myself. *"It's okay. I can let this go."*

Everything changed for me after that first breathwork retreat. That was the beginning of my spiritual awakening, and to this day, one of the most profound experiences of my entire life.

I had no idea how contributable this event would be to the rest of my life. Attending that retreat was monumental for me and continues to add value to my life. The ways I'd been holding myself back, trapped by fear instead of doing the deep emotional work, became undeniable. I felt a desire to go deeper with breathwork and to share this healing modality with others. I am so thankful I said "yes" to that retreat because it became the catalyst for everything I hold dearly.

My Entrepreneurial Journey

At the time of that retreat, I was just beginning my entrepreneurial journey as an online fitness coach. I felt my purpose was to inspire people to exercise in a fun way, feel good in their bodies, love themselves, and cultivate a healthy relationship with food. Having healed from six years of struggling with binge eating disorder, I wanted others to experience that same inner freedom.

While working with online fitness coaching clients, I noticed a pattern. They'd achieve incredible results, losing ten pounds within ten to twelve weeks, but then often plateau.. The message I received was that this plateau wasn't physical. It was emotional, and I felt called to introduce them to breathwork.

During one breathwork session, a fitness coaching client finally grieved the death of her brother, releasing years of bottled-up emotions. Afterward, she said she felt ten pounds lighter, not physically, but emotionally. Another client had a profound realization during a session: she didn't feel safe losing weight because it meant no longer fitting in with her family. Since her entire family had always been overweight, she feared feeling resented and outcasted from the family if she looked different. *"Who would I be if I came home to Thanksgiving twenty-five pounds lighter?"* she wondered. *"I'd be unrecognizable! Perhaps even unlovable!"* These are the words she told herself

The undeniable power of breathwork inspired me to go down the path of becoming a breathworker and learning how to safely guide others in a trauma-informed way. I did multiple training programs and certifications for breathwork, somatic healing, yoga, coaching, and energy work.

Nearly every coaching client I've worked with, has shared that the most powerful and profound aspect of our time together was their breathwork experiences. What I love about breathwork is that it empowers clients to go within and find their own answers. It could take someone ten years to relay every detail and micro-trauma of their life to a therapist or coach. After all, they are the ones who hold every memory and detail inside themselves.

By leading breathwork, we empower people to gain clarity, process their emotions, and heal. This practice allows individuals to shift their state of consciousness, rewriting past narratives and creating new ones for their future. Often, we overemphasize the meaning of our past experiences, allowing them to define us. The beauty of breathwork lies in its ability to empower individuals to redefine the significance of these stories.

Anyone can gain wisdom from a book and attempt to change their life, but nothing compares to the visceral experience of knowing something in your body, like the insights gained during a breathwork journey. This embodied knowledge transforms how we make decisions and present ourselves to the world. I've listened to countless podcasts and audiobooks about unconditional love, surrender, and opening the heart, but none have resonated as deeply as the insights I receive during a breathwork session. In those moments, I physically feel my heart opening, often moved to tears by a wave of trust, surrender, and unconditional love.

While my first ten breathwork sessions were the catalyst for my healing journey, my subsequent breathwork sessions have remained profoundly transformative. Healing often resembles a spiral, with new layers emerging over time. Things evolve and change because, as the saying goes, the only constant in life is change. When we allow ourselves to do this deep work, we can truly transform our lives.

What I love about breathwork is that it isn't just for deep emotional healing and cathartic moments; it can also ignite our creative life force and guide us deeper into our purpose. Breathwork has been the foundation of my business strategy every single year, and I don't see that changing anytime soon.

My friend Katie, my *"breathwork bestie,"* and I have been leading each other in breathwork sessions every week for years. This practice has been a game-changer for both of us. During many of our sessions, my intention is to gain business clarity.

I am always amazed by how many ideas and intuitive action steps come up in those breathwork sessions.

I often ask myself questions like: *Who can I support with my offerings? Who am I meant to collaborate with? What do I feel inspired to create and share?* These questions open the floodgates to endless possibilities and provide clarity, igniting my energy, passion, and enthusiasm.

When we are present and connected, we open ourselves to intuitive guidance. It's often when we try to fit ourselves into a box or follow external expectations that we feel stuck and uninspired.

If this resonates with you, I invite you to ask yourself, *"Who was I as a child?"* When I connect with my inner child, I picture myself at recess, happily digging up rocks and quartz crystals while others played four square or chased each other on the blacktop.
I remember the joy of running through the fields behind the monkey bars, chasing butterflies with a net in hand, feeling free and completely connected to nature. I even brought my butterfly net and butterfly box to school.

A few days later, other kids started showing up at recess with their own butterfly nets. I was amazed! I had no idea that I had inspired them to also play with the butterflies. I realized that I was an innovator, a trendsetter—someone who could influence others. These qualities, which first started at recess, have inspired my entrepreneurial journey.

I've always loved butterflies. They're a beautiful symbol of transformation. Just like butterflies, we go through many stages in life where we feel like we are in a metaphorical cocoon. It takes courage to emerge from that safe place, to break free from what's holding us back, and spread our wings. Breaking free from our cocoon and spreading our wings to fly means letting go of limiting beliefs and embracing all parts of ourselves—our past, our family history, and who we are today. These are powerful lessons I've learned through breathwork, lessons that have helped me transform my life.

During the breathwork sessions I lead, I often say, *"Connect to the wealth of wisdom that lives within you."*

This quote is also our tagline at Breath of Gold. I have discovered that there is a wealth of wisdom that lives within each of us, and it can be accessed through conscious breath. As someone who has always been driven by success, I used to be too hyperfocused on making money and saving money. Throughout my spiritual journey, I have realized that it doesn't matter how much money you have; truly feeling wealthy and prosperous comes from inside of ourselves.

Abundance is all around us, but to truly connect with with it, we must first appreciate and become grounded with nature. Nature is a wise teacher, showing us the abundance that exists all around usand reminding us that we already have access to everything we need.

I remember sitting in my old home office in Steamboat Springs, Colorado, and watching the beautiful aspen trees outside my window glistening and shimmering in the wind and sunlight. Their glittering leaves made me feel as if the universe was telling me that abundance was on its way.

I also remember sitting on the beach in Encinitas, California. I dug my hands into the warm sand, turning my palms up toward the sky, watching the sand cascade through my fingers. In that moment, I thought to myself, "Wow, there is such an abundance of sand." Then I looked at the waves and heard the message: "Some waves break at the shore and are gone forever, but there are always more coming. New waves are like the new opportunities that are always on their way."

Nature has been an incredible teacher of mine. To connect with our breath is to connect with the fact that we are nature. In an ever-evolving world where AI and technology are transforming at rapid paces, it is important that we never forget this. Nature is where we come from. If we allow it to be, our breath is our biggest teacher. We have everything we need at this moment within our breath.

How Being a Breathwork Facilitator Has Transformed My Life

My life has been transformed not only by my personal breathwork journey but also by witnessing the profound impact it has on others. One powerful session that stays with me involved a client named Sue, just days after Christmas. As she set her intention for the session, she shared that her husband, John, had passed away three years ago.

Despite his absence, Sue continued to honor John's memory by cooking his favorite Christmas meal, placing his picture at the dining room table, and sharing Christmas dinner with him in spirit. I was deeply touched by her devotion and could feel the strong love she still held for John.

Leading Sue through this breathwork journey was particularly meaningful for me, as I had experienced the loss of my maternal grandmother just a week before. My own journey through grief allowed me to connect more deeply with Sue's story. In that shared space, I found myself connecting more deeply with my own heart and soul as well.

As I guided Sue through that breathwork session, I experienced moments where I felt her husband John's presence in the room, almost as if he were beside me. I could also feel the presence of my own grandmother, offering comfort and support. Then, a clear image appeared in my mind's eye: John, with his hands gently resting on Sue's heart as she breathed. I was overwhelmed by the profound love they shared, a love that transcended the physical realm. It was a deeply moving experience to witness the depth of their connection, a testament to their deep connection.

At the end of the session, during the integration time, Susan was in tears as she shared her experience. She shared that she felt her late husband, John's, presence more strongly than ever before. She mentioned that the piano music I played had evoked a vivid image of John playing, just as he had during his life.

This was her first breathwork session, and I was deeply moved by the profound impact it had on her.

Leading that session was a healing and transformative experience for me as well, allowing me to witness the power of breathwork from a space-holding perspective. Susan has continued her breathwork journey, participating in sessions with me virtually every week for the past year. She has even become a contributing author to this book, sharing her own insights and experiences!

Another client who moved me powerfully was Brent, a firefighter in Reno. He shared with me that he couldn't even remember the last time he cried. His dad passed away five years ago, and he still hadn't shed a tear, despite all of the tragedy that he's seen in his life and throughout his career. He knew he deeply needed to connect to his heart, recognizing that his emotional walls were creating distance in his relationships and causing turmoil in his life. During that breathwork journey, he cried for the first time in over five years. He processed the pain of his father's death and released the pent-up emotions from the tragedies he'd witnessed as a firefighter. He felt the walls around his heart crumble and dissolve. For the first time, he felt safe enough to embrace his emotions fully.

His relationship is now stronger than ever. Since then, he has gotten married, and his wife feels deeply connected to him. They are planning to have their first child together, and he is confident that he will be an amazing father. Much of this growth is attributed to the breathwork session that helped him connect with his heart. These are just a few of the powerful journeys that have deeply moved me.

As a breathwork facilitator, I feel privileged to witness individuals opening their hearts and rewriting stories from their past.
Breathwork facilitators have the opportunity to witness people express their true selves. Breathwork is a process of returning to the heart; it is a journey towards reconnecting with the soul and becoming more of the person you have always been. This journey involves reintegrating your inner child into your present self.

I believe that God and the universe provide us with everything we need. When we observe nature, we see plants and animals coexisting in harmony, each with everything they need to thrive.

Just like them, we too are provided for. We are born with the inherent power of our breath, a tool we can harness for healing and transformation.

There are countless healing modalities available to us, some so elaborate they wouldn't fit in a suitcase. However, your breath is always with you throughout your entire waking life. It's so comforting to know this. No matter where you are, you have access to the most powerful tool for changing your emotional state and regulating your nervous system—your breath.

Our breath is nature's medicine cabinet. There's a breathwork technique for everything, from healing insomnia and easing anxiety to lowering stress levels and blood pressure. Breathwork can even help heal deep emotional wounds.

People on this earth show up differently when they're connected to their heart. It's often easier to build walls around our hearts than to confront our emotions. Many of us suppress our feelings, trying to convince ourselves we're okay instead of acknowledging how we truly feel.

Being a breathwork facilitator has given me the freedom to lead retreats around the world. Recently, I co-led a powerful breathwork journey in Colombia with Diana Rios, one of my breathwork certification graduates. Co-leading this retreat in Spanish was especially meaningful, allowing me to connect with my Latina heritage as a half-Puerto Rican woman. My Puerto Rican grandparents were the most spiritual and loving people in my life. From a young age, I felt a deep sense of love and spiritual connection with them.

I remember practicing basic questions that I was learning in my middle school Spanish class, such as "¿Cuál es tu color favorito?" which means "What is your favorite color?" I asked my abuelo, and he replied, "Rojo, porque es el color de la sangre de Jesucristo," meaning "Red, because that is the color of Jesus Christ's blood."

I remember thinking to myself, "Wow, that's profound. He has such a strong connection to God and unwavering faith."

My grandparents were devout Catholics, deeply loving and devoted to their faith. Every night, they prayed the Rosary for two hours, asking for blessings for all fifty family members. They were the happiest people I have ever met.

Despite their age, limited means, and health challenges, they smiled brighter than anyone I've ever known. Writing this brings tears to my eyes as I recall their love, generosity, and boundless kindness. They lived a beautiful life, focused on giving love and caring for others, always putting their loved ones first. Their fulfilling and impactful lives touched every member of our large Puerto Rican family, leaving a legacy of love that continues to inspire us.

I hope the story of my Puerto Rican grandpartners reminds you that to truly experience abundance, we must be willing to give. We start the cycle of abundance with generosity. It's about giving to others, connecting with our hearts, and being in the energy of love.

When I had the opportunity to lead a breathwork session in Spanish in Colombia, I deeply felt the presence of my abuela and my abuelo, who serve as my spirit guides. I imagined them holding space for me, smiling from above, filled with pride. I sensed their energy, love, and light flowing down into the breathwork circle to help heal, support, and transform the energy.

I also led a powerful breathwork session in Washington, D.C., at a business coaching event for fifty women of color. The room was filled with fellow Puerto Ricans, Latinas, Black women, Asian women, and more. I embraced the moment, allowing the words to flow through me. Afterward, many women approached me, sharing how they felt shackles break free from their wrists. They described profound experiences of rewriting their ancestral history and releasing past traumas. They felt safe to embrace wealth and express their authentic selves fully. The atmosphere was filled with movement, tears, and open hearts. Many used the session as a catalyst to pursue their goals and dreams. I continue to fly all around the world leading breathwork and training others to become trauma-informed breathwork facilitators because of the power of this work.

If you are thinking to yourself, *"Wow, these stories are amazing,"* you just wait. The stories that you are about to read in the coming chapters will move you and show you what is possible through breathwork and healing. As humans, we have learned through storytelling for thousands of years, ever since our ancestors sat around a campfire, and that's what I hope you feel reading through these stories.

There are countless books about the science of breathwork, however, there are not many that explore the profound healing possible through transformational breathwork practices. One of the main styles I teach and use is called circular connected breath. This type of breathwork has been monumental in my clients healing journeys. I've witnessed its transformative power firsthand, and that realization inspired me to write this book. I want to share these stories with you, to inspire you to step into the best version of yourself.

I saw this opportunity as a powerful catalyst for healing, both for you as the reader and for the authors. I'm looking forward to you gaining profound insights by reading these authentic and vulnerable stories. This was a profound experience for each of the authors, who integrated and processed their breathwork experiences through writing their chapters. By sharing their stories with the world, they embrace authenticity and vulnerability, deepening their own healing journey.

I hope these stories ignite your curiosity and childlike wonder, leading you to explore how breathwork can transform your life.

Breath is life. It's our gateway to healing, presence, and love. Conscious breathing practices, like breathwork, cultivate awareness and presence. When we breathe unconsciously, we tend to be less aware and fully present.

May this book inspire you to live with greater intention. In the coming chapters, you'll discover the profound experiences of others and their breathwork journeys with Breath of Gold. I hope their stories encourage you to explore the power of breathwork in your own life.

Ready to experience breathwork for yourself?

Join us online for a guided breathwork journey at

www.breathofgold.com/sunday-breathwork

Scan the QR code to Sign Up

Feeling inspired and curious about becoming a certified
breathwork facilitator?
Learn more and join our waitlist at
www.breathofgold.com/breathwork-certification-waitlist

Scan the QR code to Apply

Susan Peters

They Didn't Get To Say Goodbye

At the time of writing this chapter, I was moving through a challenging grief journey for over three years. My husband, John, experienced a severe medical crisis when his pancreas burst the day of our son's wedding in October 2020. He was hospitalized for over four months, until Valentine's Day, and unfortunately, he passed away without ever returning home.

As a result, most of our immediate family, including our grown children, their spouses, his brothers, their wives, and our grandkids either never got to see him again or only saw him once or twice during those four months. For the majority of that time, I was the only visitor allowed. There were multiple days I had to leave him. Every time I was filled with great fear that it would be the last time I would see him. As terrifying as that was, at least I am grateful that I had the chance to say goodbye to him.

On the morning of Valentine's Day, I was abruptly awakened from a deep sleep by the ringing of my phone at 4:45 a.m. A nurse practitioner was on the other end. He informed me that John had taken a turn for the worse during the night and was not responding well. He suggested that I come down to be with him, as they weren't sure how much longer he would hold on.

That morning was bitterly cold, with the temperature at -3 degrees Fahrenheit, and a massive winter storm was approaching, set to blanket the entire state of Indiana. I lived over three hours away from where John was at the hospital. My mind raced with uncertainty. I just visited him three days earlier and he seemed to be holding on. I felt torn between two choices: risk driving down in the freezing temperatures to see John or stay safely at home, hope and pray for his recovery, and wait for the weather to improve.

I decided to call the nurses' station to get their advice. Without hesitation, they urged me to come down. So, I quickly packed my bags and set out as the sun began to rise.

I arrived at the facility with hope that things had changed, but John didn't respond to my voice or the touch of my hands. They gave him extra oxygen to see if it might help. I called our three kids to inform them of what was happening. Our daughter and youngest son had the chance to talk to him while I held the phone to his ear. In response, he turned his head and tried to take off the oxygen mask. A flicker of hope ignited within me.

I shared with him how much I loved him and reassured him that he didn't need to find the words to express his love for us; we all knew it. His eyebrows moved up and down! We were connected for a brief moment. Our oldest son lived close enough to join me, and together we sat, talked, waited, and hoped for more responses, but none came.

Just before 3:00 p.m., John's heart rate and oxygen levels began to drop. The nurse and her assistant rushed in to try to stabilize him, but the numbers continued to decline. I asked if he was dying, and the nurse nodded in confirmation. Our son took John's hand while I placed one hand on his arm and the other on his head, leaning in to tell him how much we all loved him and to thank him for everything he had done for us throughout his life.

He slipped away so peacefully that I had to ask the nurse if he was truly gone. She nodded, and I said goodbye to my best friend.

Losing John was the hardest thing I have ever experienced. My journey through grief felt like an emotional roller coaster. I had no idea how I would navigate the rest of my life without him. It took me months of support to process this loss and to find a way to move forward. One of the most helpful forms of support has been through breathwork with Adrienne Rivera, the founder of Breath of Gold. Adrienne's sessions have guided me to explore deeper parts of myself in order to heal the wounds caused by grief. They have also connected me with John's spiritual presence, allowing me to embrace a new kind of relationship with him—one that serves a higher purpose. This connection has empowered me to share my story with others who have also faced loss.

I have immensely grown from this experience. It has taught me that losing someone doesn't have to mean losing the relationship with that person.

Instead, it offers a chance to view that relationship from a new perspective and to live in a new way.

When Adrienne offered me the opportunity to attend a breathwork retreat in Sedona, Arizona, I was the first to sign up! I had experienced the powerful and healing effects of breathwork and was eager to share my story through writing about my experiences during the guided process known as conscious connected breathing. Additionally, I knew that Sedona is home to one of the most powerful vortexes in the world, and I wanted to immerse myself in such a spiritual place to deepen my heart connection through breathwork.

Through this style of breathwork, I am always surprised by what unfolds during each session. Each time, something significant emerges that opens my heart in new ways and serves a greater purpose. This retreat would give me the chance to experience the breathwork journey in person for the first time. As soon as Adrienne officially opened registration, I signed up and booked my flights. Within weeks, I was on my way to Sedona!

As I drove into Sedona from the west side for the first time in the late afternoon, I marveled at the stunning red rock formations highlighted by the sun. The beauty of the landscape took my breath away, and I found myself overwhelmed with emotions, bringing me to tears more than once as I got closer. It felt like a profound honor to be in such a sacred place, surrounded by these expansive rock formations that stretched across the horizon. Just witnessing them and realizing that they have existed for over 300 million years instilled in me a sense of grounding, solidity, and security.

The first day of the retreat focused on getting to know one another through sharing and grounding. We gathered outside in a garden-like setting on a beautiful piece of land adorned with trees, flowers, stones, and a flowing creek. We participated in an incredible sound healing session led by Shawn LaFountain. Later, Adrienne guided us through a two-hour breathwork journey, assisted by her husband, Darren Thomas who provided support to the four retreat attendees: Tracey-Ann Rose, Amy Quinn, Shawn, and myself. (You will hear about each of their journeys soon.)

As the music began and Adrienne guided us, I found myself in a space with my paternal grandfather. He was gently holding my hands and kindly smiling at me. Suddenly, a flood of emotions washed over me and my heart felt heavy. I remembered having the chance to talk to my grandfather before he passed away. Although I was only four years old, I could still recall that phone call. In this moment, I also remembered that my grandchildren never had the chance to say goodbye to their Grandpa John, whom they loved dearly and who loved them immensely.

The weight of this realization hit me hard, as if I could feel their overwhelming sadness and profound loss. My heart overflowed with grief as I envisioned our children, family members, and friends who also didn't get to say goodbye. I cried out loud, imagining the pain each person experienced upon receiving the devastating news of his passing, along with the lost opportunity for a final visit and farewell. I felt their pain intensely, almost as if it were processing through me and into the earth.

As I lay on the ground sobbing, I felt Adrienne gently hold my hands, allowing me to release the excruciating truth over and over again. I whispered, "They didn't get to say goodbye! They didn't get to say goodbye! They didn't get to say goodbye!"

As Adrienne embraced me and allowed my emotions to flow, I wept for quite a while until a new realization emerged. Suddenly, I felt as if my breathing was connected to John's final breaths. In that moment, I understood that at a deeper soul level, everyone who was not physically present was actually there in spirit. Each of us was present with John, sharing those final breaths with him, enveloped in the tender love he inspired as he gently left this world. I cannot fully explain how healing it was to connect in this way and view the death of someone so loved by so many in a new light. It was a special opportunity to deeply feel and acknowledge the love that each person held for him.

On the second day of the retreat, I learned so much about trusting the unknown, releasing what is unnecessary, and holding on to what is truly valuable. We all hiked together to and from Cathedral Rock, as well as the 4,967 feet up to the Vortex at the summit.

As our group climbed higher and higher towards the Vortex, I felt both inspired and strengthened. I had to concentrate with each step I took, pushing through my doubts, fears, and perceived physical limits. Everyone was climbing, so I kept climbing too. Although we each had to navigate the rocks on our own, we kept an eye on one another, lending a hand, taking breaks, and motivating each other. I was learning valuable life lessons from the experience.

I realized that no matter what challenges we face, we are stronger together. We can support one another through moments of doubt and fatigue. Climbing is hard work, requiring concentration, determination, strength, coordination, and willpower. Our goal was to reach the top, and we accomplished it together!

Life is full of unknowns, much like our hike, which presented various terrains. Our trek included steep rocks, narrow spaces, a creek with slippery stones, thorns, downed trees, and grass that scratched our legs. As I walked, I learned that the more I trusted those around me, the more I could trust myself to reach new heights. I began to understand that I could navigate through anything, accomplish my goals, heal from challenges, learn valuable lessons, and even enjoy the journey!

Participating in the breathwork journey after climbing and hiking allowed me to reach a new level of emotional connection. Climbing to the Vortex stirred deep feelings within me, which surfaced later during breathwork. This experience helped me heal emotions I hadn't realized were lingering.

While lying next to Tracey-Ann, Amy, and Shawn, I could sense their emotional processes and the energy in the space we shared. Being together in this sacred environment intensified our emotions and provided a greater opportunity for release.

On Day 2, as Adrienne led us through the breathwork, we shared moments of simultaneous tears, laughter, and peaceful stillness. We formed a deeper connection, letting go of what no longer served us while remaining open to what we each needed to receive.

It never occurred to me that I was carrying the weight of extra pain and sadness from those who never got to say goodbye to John. Through the power of my breath, the music, and Adrienne's guiding words, I felt opened up to the energy of the entire group. As we spent those two hours together, I gained a new perspective on what I was holding onto, recognizing that I needed to release the sadness and pain that was not mine to carry. This experience also provided me with new insights and empathy for my family members, who may still need to process their own grief and find healing.

During Saturday's two-hour afternoon breathwork session, I felt myself going into a deep state of connection energetically with John. His presence was palpable near my hands; I could sense his life force energy flowing through them. This connection tied me to my diamond engagement ring and wedding band, which I still wear—rings he had lovingly placed on my finger. In that moment, I felt that his love for me remains strong and will always be a part of me.

I then felt my two hands come together, with the rings on my left hand touching a special heart ring on my right hand. I had chosen that heart ring for myself in a ceremony I created to "marry my own heart" after John's passing, as a symbol of fully loving myself.

In my heart, I sensed John saying he would be with me as I moved forward to live my life in new ways. It felt as if he took my hand in his, and at that exact moment, I actually felt physical hands grasping mine. Darren, who was co-leading the breathwork, happened to reach out to gently hold my hands since they were raised in the air. A song that was on a predetermined playlist played, and in that moment, the lyrics sang, "Hold my hands!" I exclaimed in total amazement, "Oh wow!" If I hadn't already been lying down, I probably would have fallen over! The timing was astounding, and I knew it was a beautiful message of love from John to encourage me to keep moving forward.

I felt like John's spirit inspired Darren to use his hands to hold mine on his behalf. As I felt John's energy holding my hands, I sensed him giving me extra encouragement to use writing as a way to "hold the hands" of those experiencing loss and grief.

I could also feel John's presence around my legs and feet, as if he were steadying me to provide support as I began to walk this new path, just as I always took the time to care for his feet while he walked his journey on this earth.

On the third day of the retreat, we did our breathwork journey outside! It felt so much more expansive yet at the same time, deeply grounding. The sounds of nature—the flowing river, singing birds, and the gentle wind—blended harmoniously with the music, voices, and instruments, as if they were all playing together. The subtle movement of the wind brushed gently against my face and hands, helping me to be more present in the moment. The wind became my teacher; it showed me how effortlessly things can shift. It brought in blessings for me to receive and carried away what I needed to let go of. It reminded me of my true presence in the now and connected me to a greater awareness of those who love me. I also became more aware of the group energy as it interacted with the wind, swirling around us with varying intensities, shifting back and forth from person to person.

I began to reconnect with John's presence energetically. This time, I felt his energy as it was on his final day alive, just before he transitioned from this world. Even though his physical presence was fading, his spiritual presence grew stronger. I sensed that he truly understood what each person who loved him was experiencing as they processed the news on his last day of life. He was there with each of them, offering comfort as they faced the pain of separation.

It became increasingly clear to me that my trip to Sedona was teaching me to embody valuable life lessons through the powerful combination of breathwork and physical movement toward a goal. Each step I took during the hike up Cathedral Rock left a lasting impression on my mind, body, and soul. I was able to keep moving forward with seemingly little effort by focusing on climbing one step at a time, without looking too far ahead or worrying about what lay next.

"What if we lived like this?" I pondered. What if we could fully embrace the present moment, without stressing about the next "twenty rocks we need to climb," the future challenges we might face, or the uncertainties ahead? Instead, what if we concentrated on the rock we are currently climbing—the rock of the present moment? With this perspective, anything becomes possible!

This reflection led me to consider the suffering we often create when we have to say goodbye to one another. What if we adopted this same approach of being truly present during these farewells, whether they are brief, prolonged, or a final goodbye through death? In essence, we are all present in this moment, which means we are inherently connected as one in the now.

This Sedona breathwork retreat helped me realize that when John died, he did not die alone. Although the only people physically present in the room with him were our son, a nurse, an assistant, and myself, I learned that the souls of all those who loved him were also very present in their higher spirit form during those final moments, as well as in all the moments of perceived separation. For me, that connection became undeniable once I experienced my raised hands being touched by John reaching out in spirit, Darren reaching out physically, and the words "hold my hands" being sung at the exact same time. This made me aware that none of us are ever really separate from each other. That moment deepened my understanding of Oneness and presence in a way I will never forget.

I have witnessed the loss of someone I loved very much, and I understand the pain it caused those who could not be physically present. I know how hard it was for those who didn't get the chance to personally visit and express their feelings as John lived out his last days. However, after my amazing experience at Adrienne's breathwork retreat, I now believe that it is often in those moments of seeming disconnection that we are actually more united than apart. There exists a connection at a spiritual level that is akin to what one experiences at the Vortex on Cathedral Rock. While I was there, I could feel the spirits of all who had climbed and stood in that space. The challenge and mastery of the climb create a profound connection at the top.

That hike was a powerful continuation of the deep spiritual journey that I felt with John. As I was climbing up the rocks, it reminded me of his "final climb,"--his last few breaths on this Earth. I felt that as John lay dying, it was as if he was making his final climb up the rocks to the Vortex. We were climbing with him.

As we all stood in spirit at the top with the wind blowing around us and our breaths combined with the wind, John took his final breath as we inhaled with him. As we exhaled, he gained his spiritual wings as we sent him on his way into the most beautiful expanse of pure peace and pure joy and pure love! At that moment, we ALL had a chance to say, *"Goodbye!"*

My breathwork experiences with Adrienne and Breath of Gold have taught me so much.

(1). we don't have to be afraid of death or of not being there with our loved ones when they die. We can free ourselves of any fear or guilt for not being able to be physically there, because we are always present energetically and spiritually to each other.

(2). none of us die alone. We can all learn from John that ironically we are more expanded and connected spiritually at the time of death and can actually still be present to each other even though many miles may separate us. We don't need to be afraid that no one will be with us when we die, AND we need not feel guilty if we are unable to be with our loved ones when they die. We are all together in spirit.

(3). we are not disconnected from our loved ones after they die. Death cannot separate us! They are always with us and are always looking for ways to connect with us. Breathwork is one of THE most powerful ways that we can open up to feeling that deep connection with our loved ones who have passed.

So the next time you feel like you are afraid or alone or disconnected during a time of loss, turn to the power of your breath and remember – *You Are Never Alone!*

Shawn LaFountain

It's All Within You

"You had a stroke."

I laughed in disbelief as the doctor showed me the image from the CT scan and explained what was happening. "But only old people have strokes," I protested. "There's no way!" It was March 10th, 2022. The next day, I was in the hospital, being wheeled into an operating room and prepared for surgery to remove a tumor nearly the size of my fist from my brain. Little did I know at the time, this experience would be a major catalyst in my spiritual awakening.

To make a long story short, the surgery was successfu. I recovered quickly and within a matter of weeks, I was released from the hospital. After a month of chemo and radiation treatments, I went straight back to my day job and I thought my life would slowly but surely return to normal. But it turns out God had a different plan for me. About a month after returning to my regular programing, I was sitting in my office when all of a sudden, I found myself struggling to catch my breath. For no apparent reason, I was huffing and puffing, trying to take the deep breath my body craved, but I could never fully satisfy my need for air. It felt as if I was suffocating, drowning in an endless sea of air. It was one of the most frightening experiences of my life. Was I really doing to die now? Really? After surviving brain surgury and a cancer diagnosis? Since this was at the tail end of the COVID-19 pandemic and my immune system was vulnerable due to chemotherapy and radiation treatments, I feared the worst. So, yet again, I found myself back in the emergency room. After being poked, prodded, scanned, and evaluated, the doctors couldn't find anything physically wrong with me. The only logical explanation was that I had experienced my first panic attack.

That night, on the ride home from the hospital, I heard a clear inner voice declare, "You need to learn to control your breath." At that point in my life, the only brreathwork I had ever heard of or experienced was the Wim Hof method. However, I didn't yet have a genuine relationship with my breath.

Having my first panic attack ignited a deep desire within me to cultivate that relationship. Over the next two years, I fully immersed myself in the world of breathwork. Following this path of self-healing through breathwork led me to sound healing, reiki, and many other holistic healing modalities. All of these led to miraculous physical healing and numerous eye-opening experiences. However, the breathwork journey of self-discovery that unfolded over three days at the Breath of Gold retreat in Sedona led by Adrienne unlocked something profound within me. It feels almost too big to express in words, but I will do my best. Walking away from this experience, I feel a permanent and unshakable shift in my body at a cellular level. This shift unlocked a deeper layer rof self-knowing, self-trust, self-forgiveness, freedom, and creativity which has led to an overall sense of returning home within myself. The following is the story of my inner journey and how it all unfolded.

Trust

From the start of the first breathwork session of the retreat, I received a message I was not expecting at all. However, since I set the intention beforehand to surrender to whatever arose during this journey, when I received this message, I surrendered to the experience to see where it would take me.

The message was:

"Trust yourself. You already have all the answers inside you. You always have."

After receiving this message, I felt enveloped by a violet flame, and suddenly, my heart felt like it exploded open. My heart space transformed into a radiating toroidal field of powerful, loving energy that surrounded my chest. This was a sensation I had only experienced once before, during a Reiki healing session right after my initial release from the hospital after brain surgery. However, this time, my heart felt so open that it seemed to merge with the hearts of everyone in the room. A profound, grounding feeling of love washed over me—both in my body and subtly surrounding and pervading through everything in the room at the same time.

It was a true experience of oneness; I had only grasped this concept intellectually before that moment. After breathing and basking in this beautiful feeling of grounded love and unity, we were guided to connect with our inner child and ask them what they saw in us now.

I saw the younger version of myself from 8th grade, the little me who had just begun playing music at school. As soon as he saw my present self, his eyes lit up. He was so excited to see me now and exclaimed, "You are badass!" All I could do was cry and hug myself as I realized that I am exactly where I need to be and that my past selves are proud of the person I have become.

Reflecting on the younger versions of myself, a vivid image of my ten-year-old self flashed into my mind. At that age I lived next to a large wooded area that I would often explore after school. Those woods provided me with an incredible sense of freedom as a child. Some of my fondest memories from my youth are of venturing into those woods alone, feeling as though I knew every part of it like the back of my hand.

However, one day I strayed a little farther than usual and stumbled upon a large fallen tree. Intrigued, I climbed onto it and sat there for a while, enjoying the sounds of nature from what felt like the biggest bench I'd ever encountered. When I finally decided to head home, I realized I couldn't quite recall how I had reached that fallen tree. Panic set in as I looked around, unsure of which way to go to find my way back.

Then, a sudden wave of confidence washed over me, and I chose a direction to head home. I didn't take a straight path back, but I focused on what I knew and trusted—my intuition. Before dark, I made it home safe and sound. This experience reminded me that I am divinely guided, and as long as I trust my intuition, *I will always find my way.*

By the end of my first breathwork session, the seemingly random message I received at the beginning became clear. Not only can I trust myself; I must trust myself! Even when the exact path isn't clear, I can rely on my intuition to help me take the next step.

This new understanding sparked visions of how I could apply my rediscovered sense of trust in my life right now. I began to explore ideas about stepping into my power using the knowledge and skills I already possess. The only question that remains is whether I will trust myself and take that next step. After this experience, I can confidently say, "Yes!"

My journey of insight, self-reflection, and rediscovering my inner light has deepened with each breathwork session, adding new elements to my personal healing. I witnessed my inner child and past versions of myself bringing forth memory after memory, helping me let go of the emotional baggage I didn't even realize I was holding onto. One of the most transformative moments in this process came when I received the message: "You have to forgive yourself before you can step into your power." At first, I didn't grasp the significance of this profound channeled message. Over the past two years, I had done a lot of inner work, navigating through self-forgiveness as well as forgiving others. However, as I continued to breathe deeply and reflect on this idea, the true meaning of the message became clear to me.

Forgiveness

As a child, I had a deep appreciation for and connection to music. Growing up in a time just before the advent mp3s and digital streaming, I enjoyed listening to music on the radio. I have fond memories of waiting to hit the record button on my tape recorder at just the right moment to cut out commercials and DJ commentary. I spent hours creating playlists of my favorite songs. My love for music continued through elementary school, where I joined the school band, playing flute and percussion. In high school, I played drumset in a punk rock band, competing in battles of the bands and performing at birthday parties with my closest friends, who all dreamed that we would become famous rock stars one day. I even earned a music education degree in college and worked as a marching band director for four years as a young adult. However, at one point, I decided that teaching music was no longer for me, and I walked away from music entirely for nearly ten years.

While lying on the floor in Sedona and breathing deeply, it struck me that music had been my closest friend for as long as I could remember. In that moment, music became more than just enjoyable sounds or vibrations. It transformed into a living, breathing, conscious being. I felt the loss that this dear old friend had experienced when I walked away all those years ago. Each note, each instrument, each harmony, and each melody felt like a friend waiting faithfully and patiently for my return. At that moment, they didn't judge me for neglecting them for so long. Instead, I realized that music had missed me just as much, if not more, than I had missed it during the years I turned away.

Then, either through divine timing, intuition, or luck, Adrienne knelt down and hugged me right at the moment I felt my soul reuniting with music in complete forgiveness and love. I cried as I forgave myself for ever turning away from my dear old friend, music. I could feel all the walls of self-doubt, shame, and regret surrounding music melting away with that embrace. I experienced a complete return of the innocent love and connection I had felt for music as a child and young adult. It felt like the embrace of a long-lost friend or loved one—a return to home within myself. In that moment, I finally understood what I had been holding onto and what I hadn't been able to forgive myself for. Allowing myself the grace of forgiveness peeled back another layer that had been holding me back from stepping into my personal power and fully expressing my creativity.

Lying there on the floor with tears in my eyes, I made a promise to myself and to my friend, the music that is ever-present inside me: I will never turn my back on you again.

Creativity

According to my human design chart, I am a manifesting generator. Additionally, I identify as an Enneagram Type Three, known as "The Achiever." This combination often leads me to measure my life by significant milestones and accomplishments, such as competing in state music competitions during high school, receiving a prestigious performance-based music scholarship in college, becoming the drumline section leader of a Division 1 drum corps, and graciously overcoming a brain cancer diagnosis.

However, focusing solely on major achievements can be exhausting and tends to create a sense of distraction, as I am always searching for the next challenge to conquer. While I take pride in my past accomplishments, I often find myself questioning their purpose. In moments like these, self-doubt creeps in, and I start to wonder what I might still need to achieve or pursue. This line of thinking frequently leaves me feeling stuck, which is one of the most frustrating states for a manifesting generator. As I approached the weekend of the breathwork retreat, I realized I was deeper in this sense of "stuckness" than I had initially understood.

On the second day of the retreat, I began to feel a shift in my energy as that stagnant feeling started to move again. As I lay on the floor breathing deeply, my sacral chakra activated, and I realized that my entire life has been a spiritual journey. Instead of measuring my life by physical achievements, I was reminded of the significant spiritual milestones I have experienced. I recalled having my first out-of-body experience when I was around eleven years old. I felt my true essence floating above my body, observing it and wondering why this body was chosen for me, and why I was given this life at this particular time.

This experience has followed me throughout my life, fueling my genuine curiosity about the mind-body-spirit connection and how it affects my interactions with others. I then envisioned my first psychedelic experience—the first time I smoked weed in college. I ended up lying on a historic brick street on campus, exclaiming, "It's everywhere!" My friend, trying to calm me down, kept asking what "it" was. I could only respond, "It is everything! And it's everywhere!" At that moment, I didn't fully comprehend the significance of what I was experiencing, but looking back now, I recognize that it was my first profound realization of the interconnectedness of all that exists, both seen and unseen. Lying under the stars in my small college town, where light pollution was minimal, I was overwhelmed by that experience, unlike any I had encountered before.

I then received a glimpse of a memory about a profound experience on the day my son was born, where I felt an undeniable connection, as if we had known each other across many lifetimes.

This feeling was followed by a memory of the moment I met my spirit guide after practicing a simple box breathing exercise. I recalled listening as he explained how he had always been with me, guiding me during my meditation journey ten years prior.

Next, I remembered the moment right before I went in for brain surgery to remove a tumor. I felt the presence of a thousand angels sweeping their wings down my body, sending incredible waves of energy from my head to my feet. This presence fostered a sense of peace and indescribable calm throughout my entire being. I was reminded of the moment after surgery when I heard one of the angels whisper in my ear, "You are healed."

Following these spiritual milestones flashing through my mind, a voice inside me exclaimed, "See?! Your life has always been a spiritual journey." It suddenly became clear that I didn't need to focus on specific outcomes. The outcome is, and will always be, the ever-present creative expression of who I truly am. I realized that this moment-by-moment creative expression is the purpose of my existence. A sense of freedom washed over me as I embraced this new understanding, feeling safe to explore my creativity at my own pace. For as long as I can remember, my life has been driven by external, material outcomes. I had this need for tangible results to feel happy and accomplished. This realization was a wild awakening for me. In that moment, I visualized my sacral energy center opening up into a dark, earthy orange vortex, radiating a foot above my lower stomach. The energy pulsed as it rotated into a beautiful spiral. I was filled with overwhelming joy and ease. All I could do was laugh and cry as I allowed myself to rest in this feeling of joyful, creative freedom.

Integration

By the final day of the retreat, I wasn't sure if it was possible to have any more breakthroughs. I had received so many insights already and I was feeling great. My body, mind, and spirit were already feeling refreshed, whole, and complete. As I lay down outside for that final breathwork session, I truly had no expectations. My intention was to release any lingering self-doubt and make the final step into my personal power.

Lying on the ground outside, breathing deeply by the flowing water on a breezy day in Sedona, I felt free. I allowed myself to feel proud of all of the work I had done to lead myself to that moment. I could feel the energy in my body building and the power grow within my solar plexus, just as I had intended at the start of the session. Toward the middle of the session, however, I had a sudden vision and insight that I was not expecting.

As a certified chakra energy healer and meditation teacher, I am very familiar with the energy centers of the body and the ascribed function of each. But, in that moment, I had the realization of a fundamental flaw in my training and work with these energy centers. Up to that moment, I had been treating each energy center of the body as if they were mutually exclusive. I was living as if I had to choose each moment to act from the heart OR from an energy of personal power.

The message I received at that moment was, "You can't fully express yourself through love without letting the light of your power shine." I then received a vision of my heart center lighting up bright green, along with my solar plexus as a bright, golden yellow. I have seen these energy centers before with my inner vision. However, this time, I didn't see them as two separate and exclusive energies. In that moment, they became one continuous stream of energy, each color slowly integrating and changing into the next. The feeling of personal power and love combined into one feeling activated within me. Two individual energies that I had felt before, suddenly emerged as one and became a greater, even more powerful force within me.

While it may be true that we can choose to act from a primary energy in each moment, we can also choose to live from an energetically integrated perspective, whole and complete. Meaning, everything we do can come from a place of full expression of ourselves, with every action coming from a place of love, personal power, grounded safety, creativity, intuition, and divine inspiration. It inspires me to think of what the world would be like if more people were able to live from this fully integrated, aligned, and activated energy.

I believe this is how we are meant to live and after this retreat experience, I deeply know that part of the reason I am here on this earth at this time is to help awaken this energy in others.

Following My Calling

When I was diagnosed with brain cancer,my doctor said that statistically, I would be dead right now. My heart overflows with gratitude and resolve as I write this chapter because it is no secret that we live in a world in desperate need of healing, and through this experience, I know I have something to offer to the world with the extra time I have been given.

Breathwork has been life-changing for me. It has unlocked a whole new world of soul-level healing. And now, as a certified Breath of Gold facilitator, I am so proud to have the skills and knowledge to facilitate the same transformation in the lives of others. Breathwork has been a perfect compliment to the other healing modalities of sound healing, reiki, and meditation that I have adopted and become certified in over the course of my own healing journey. It gives me great pleasure to share these skills and hold space for those who are ready to step through the door of their own personal transformation. Whether it be a cancer diagnosis or any other difficult season of life, the journey to true healing starts and ends with a deep soul-level knowing that everything you need to heal is already within you.

Tracey-Ann Rose

The Journey Back to Myself

May 2nd, 2024: One Day Before the Retreat

Hurriedly, I rushed out the back door, stepping into the thick Georgia humidity.

My husband, Jason, kissed me goodbye in the driveway as we watched the black SUV from Lyft speed past the pickup point.

I waved after it, dragging my oversized suitcase behind me. I was only going to be gone for five days, but it felt like a lifetime before I would see my family again.

The chorus of "I miss you, Mommy" and "I love you" from my three-year-old, Ian, and six-year-old, Noah, only made the time apart feel longer.

I climbed into the backseat of the car.

My heart ached preemptively for the moments I would miss: feeling my little ones' arms wrapped around my legs as they squeezed, laughing with my husband in bed as we talked about our day, and the creature comforts that my Taurus Rising sign so regularly found security in.

I felt nervous—which made sense.

Logically, I knew I was on my way to a lot of firsts.

My first time traveling across the country alone.
My first retreat.
My first time co-writing a book.
My first series of two-hour long breathwork sessions.

Intuitively, I knew my world was about to be blown wide-open.

It felt like a thrumming underneath my feet or sometimes sudden chills. I could sense change was imminent, but how would it transpire? I had no clue. I was excited and terrified.

The current astrology reflected my inner knowing.

On that day, Pluto, the planet that governs power dynamics, transformation, and the unconscious mind, went into retrograde.

If you're not familiar with astrology, retrogrades are a chance for us to internally process the themes or lessons of the planet stationing retrograde. During this period, it's supportive to ask ourselves, "Where are we giving away our power or holding ourselves back from much needed changes in our daily life? "

It's a time when deep truths come to light—not to be shunned or cast off—but to be held, seen, and honored. Even if they were ugly. Even if they hurt. Even if they changed everything.

As I waved goodbye to my family from the tinted windows, I etched the emotional memory into my body.

I reminded myself of what my coach, Alyssa Harris, often says: "This is happening for you, not to you."

I smiled as a shiver traveled up my spine. I knew that when I returned, I would never be the same again.

April 4th, 2024: 30 Days Before the Retreat

When people ask how I heard about the retreat, I tell them it all happened in a divine convergence.

Thirty days ago, I walked through the palatial lobby of the Willard Continental Hotel clutching my phone.

It was my first business conference, and I was ecstatic and nervous as hell. I could feel the electricity and excitement. I was finally going to meet this community of like-minded women of color and allies who believed in equity for all through entrepreneurship. Then doubt crept in.

What if they didn't like me? Worse yet, what if I made a fool of myself and tanked my business?
What if I never signed another client again?

I took a deep breath and set my mind to the task at hand—signing up for bonus activities provided for by the conference.

Barre class? Check. Free headshots? Definitely. Breathwork? I paused.

I'd been searching for a breathwork retreat. None of them felt quite right. And now this opportunity for a thirty-minute session appeared.

As a Certified Reiki Master Teacher, I knew the power of intentional breath. I used light breathwork to prepare clients to relax prior to our work together.

But a thirty-min session of breathwork?

I thought about the transformation it could create as it united the soul, mind, and body; the revelatory images and messages I would receive from my guides; and the vulnerability that would inevitably accompany it.

Was I prepared to potentially ugly-cry in front of all these other business owners? Would they think I was unhinged? My stomach churned.

I didn't just want to experience longform breathwork, it was a need.

The need felt uncomfortable. I had felt and followed my intuition for almost ten years, but in times of high stress, it tore me apart. I felt like the symbol of the astrological sign, Pisces: two fish attached at the tail, swimming in opposite directions.

Growing up, having emotional needs felt like a luxury. If it didn't directly sustain my life and lead to financial gain, it felt like a hobby and a distraction. Living in a household with lower income, and as a child of an immigrant, I learned to move my emotional needs to the backburner.

My emotional needs were to be fulfilled later. When everyone else was taken care of...

After I comforted my husband through a hard day of work.

Or supported my clients through energy work and intuitive guidance in our sessions.

Or held space for my sons to grow into the version of themselves that they aspired to be.

I decided that my needs were to be taken care of in the early morning, the late night, and on certain days of the week.

But even then, they were highly structured to benefit my family—even if it was to my detriment.

Discomfort or not, right here, right now, this emotional need would not go unmet. I signed my name on the list of Breathwork session participants, other people's perceptions be damned.

April 5th, 2024: 29 Days Before the Retreat

Finally, the evening for breathwork arrived.

As soon as I laid down alongside fifty plus business women, I felt my energy settle into stillness and tranquility. Adrienne Rivera, the breathwork facilitator, guided the room of people on a journey of self-understanding.

Her voice filled the room as she spoke into the microphone. "What is currently holding you back in your business? What are you afraid to achieve? What are you afraid to lose?" she asked.

The tears flowed freely. I saw my uncle, who had passed years before, encouraging me to trust my journey as a first generation Jamaican-American. He had paved the way to financial freedom, and it was my time to follow in his footsteps.

I saw my grandma, who had passed away my freshman year of college. She was always my biggest fan. Most of the praise I received growing up had come from academics—reading at the age of two, starting school a year early, skipping a grade, graduating from college at twenty years old.

Grandma didn't care about that. She loved me for the things I wasn't good at, the things I excelled at, and everything in between. She gave me the message that the same unconditional love is still available to me—if I'm open to it.

I saw my five year old self. The version of myself who saw symbols and significance in the smallest of details, like a swirl of lotion. The self who led group meditations with my friends on the elementary school playground before I knew what meditation was. The part of me that always felt a deeply rooted desire to help those who were neglected feel seen, loved, and valued.

When the breathwork journey was over, I was laughing. The joy, the grief, the love! It all intermingled into a beautiful layer of clarity.

I had to experience more.

That night I spoke to my coach, Alyssa. She confirmed everything that my vision had told me.

It was time to claim my power, to stop fearing rejection, and start being vulnerable. The right people and opportunities would inherently come to me. I had to stop worrying about what other people thought of me, and start focusing on the reasons I was there. To learn, connect, and increase my positive impact on others.

I knew it was worth it, but still when it came to receiving hot seat coaching (advice about a specific problem in your business), my nerves returned.

I stepped up to the mic. I could feel the room full of eyes on me. The nervous sweat flowed freely and I found myself avoiding eye contact with the event host, Dielle Charon, who was coaching me.

"What if I can't effectively communicate what I do in my marketing?" I asked.

Dielle looked at me. I had asked this question before.

"What's coming up for you?" she countered.

My eyes started to sting.

"It's just that all of you are so brilliant, and I'm..I'm..not." The tears flowed down my cheeks.

Dielle looked at me. *"You're brilliant, too."*

The room began to chime in. Camille, a friend I had coached online, even demanded a mic to tell me how wonderful and helpful I'd been to her. It ended with a giant group hug. A definite high.

I started to feel on top of the world. Maybe being vulnerable wasn't a weakness. Perhaps it was revolutionary. An act of radical self-expression.

As the conference wrapped, several women came up to me to share how my openness inspired them, helped them feel less alone.

On the flight home, I felt powerful. What an experience to be valued—not for what I could give to others, but just for being who I am.

I felt a new level of confidence as a business owner. I had a plan on how to revamp my sales messaging, an invitation to be a guest on a summit, and new friends I was excited to get to know even better.

Then the vulnerability hangover hit.

What if all the nice things those women said were just pity?

What's inspiring about you? You're just a baby business owner.

They were probably just saying that to be nice.

When they arose, I deepened my breath, reminding myself of the visions I'd seen during the breathwork session.

I am meant to be here. I am powerful. I belong. I'm here to change lives.

Days later, scrolling through Instagram, I noticed a reel from Adrienne. She was hosting a Breathwork and Book-writing Retreat in Sedona, Arizona.

For several years, I had received signs from my guides (divine beings who protect, support, and guide you throughout your life) to write a book. Between people telling me they'd love to see me write one, or connecting to a coach for bestselling book writers online, and almost every energy reader mentioning it in readings since I was twenty-five, I knew I was destined to write one.

Then my perfectionism would kick in with all the reasons I wasn't ready.

You don't know enough.

What would you even write about?

Who would listen to you?

I breathed in the confidence that I gained from the conference's breathwork session, and direct messaged Adrienne.

She explained that we would write about our experience at the retreat. It was all about doing breathwork, allowing the intuitive guidance to come to you, and simply sharing that journey. No perfectionism required.

Twenty-four days later, I was on a flight to Sedona.

May 3rd, 2024: Day 1 of the Retreat

I lugged my oversized suitcase, throwing it in the back of my white rental car.

I had flown into Phoenix, Arizona, the night before, and it was time for the two-hour drive to the retreat lodge in Sedona. I could feel my nerves rising again.

My Reiki mentor once told me that there are four portals to the divine: Music, light (usually dim light), smell, and breath.

I decided to lean into the breath and music. I connected my phone to the car's bluetooth and put all my songs on shuffle—a practice I compare to tarot cards. When you do this with intention, every song is a message from your guides (spiritual beings who support you throughout your life).

And my spirit guides came through.

I could feel the energy shift to a higher vibration as I drove past the dusty red mountains punctuated by the sage-green bushes.

"Karma Chameleon" by Culture Club came on. I smiled. It always reminded me of Grandma. She would sit and watch me perform the whole of the cassette tape, smiling and clapping the entire time.

Then *"Driving Through a Dream"* by Andrew McMahon came on. Mike was here.

Mike was my boyfriend during my sophomore year of high school. He was known around high school for always wearing green, having long hair, and doing whatever the hell he wanted. He had an undeniable charisma that even the teachers respected, allowing him to get away with way more than the average student.

Even after we broke up, we remained friends. Mike was always my cheerleader, my protector, and a trusted confidante.

Mike passed away tragically in his late twenties. The news report said he was driving the wrong way down a one-way highway at night, with his headlights off, intoxicated.

After his passing, I accidentally started to tap into my mediumship capabilities. I'd be in the middle of a session, describing an energy that was coming in, and they'd tell me that person was dead. It taught me that mediumship is just reading the energy of someone who's passed away. But still, it felt a little too "woo woo"— even for me.

When Mike died, mediumship became a comfort to me. It wouldn't bring him back, but at least we could still talk, still connect. He was the same as in life. His spirit would give me messages, guidance, and support.

Through the song, I felt his joyful and mischievous spirit riding in the car with me. I wanted to connect with him, but I didn't want to hear the song.

"Connect with me another way," I said, and skipped the song.

Finally, I arrived in Sedona. A little roundabout led me to the road the lodge was on. Plastic barricades blocked the way. A man in a neon yellow vest motioned for me to do a U-turn.

I rolled down my window. "I'm here for a retreat?" I said.

The man waved me through.

Back to the breath.

It was time to trust the messages from my first breathwork session with Adrienne at the conference.

I am meant to be here. I am powerful. I belong. I'm here to change lives.

The lodge was breathtaking. As I opened my car door, I was met with soothing meditation music emanating from the home. At the threshold were Adrienne, a support person from the Breath of Gold, and Darren (Adrienne's husband, who was also supporting.)

I rushed to unlock the trunk and prepared my core for the duress of trying to pull my giant rollie suitcase out of the trunk.

"I got that for you," said Darren.

"Thank you," I said. I already felt supported and safe.

Upon entering the threshold, Adrienne handed me a lime-green cucumber smoothie, and a welcoming embrace.

"I feel like a star!" I said.

"You are," she laughed.

From there, it was a cascade of love and peace. I met Shawn, another participant and CEO of SoundStream. He was surrounded with what I can only describe as a cacophony of instruments. Drums, flutes, and singing bowls were artfully placed on a rug. Incense burned on the fireplace.

This is my kinda place!

Adrienne showed me to my room. It was large but cozy. Vast and welcoming. And with a gorgeous tub that I knew I could soak in all day, if I let myself.

The rest of the participants came together, Sue and Amy. Sue is a wonderful woman, a bestselling author with a fiery energy and a zest for life. Amy is a strong, warm woman who works with horses and travels the world.

It was wonderful to be surrounded by such interesting people who were dedicated to their personal growth and so willing to go deep right away.

We sat down in the backyard and had an intention setting exercise. Why were we all here?

When it was time for me to share my intention for the retreat, I mentioned my intrusive thoughts. I shared that I felt they originated from wanting to hold myself back from something. Success, broadening my world, something. Either way, I could feel them holding me back in my business too, and I wanted to uncover the source and rewire my neural pathways, so I could take action on what I knew to be my purpose.

Soon after, we did our first two-hour breathwork session. Two hours was going to be quite the jump for me, but I was prepared and I was determined to do the deep work of transformation that I knew the Pluto retrograde called for. I knew there would be more love, self-acceptance, and magnetism on the other side.

Disclaimer: From here on out, most of what you'll read is channeled. I hope it shifts your life even a fraction of the way these messages shifted mine.

In my first two-hour experience, I was taken back in time to see my grandmother giving birth to my mom. In the vision, my mom's father was nowhere to be found. Just like in real life.

Then I was shown my mother giving birth to me in a hospital room. She cried happily as she held me. Once again, there was no father present. My biological father never wanted me to be born and he wasn't known for concessions.

Then I was taken back to giving birth to my first child, Noah. As I was pushing, Jason passed out on the floor. When he came to, he said, "I'm alright," and touched the back of his head. Blood coated his fingers. The nurses rushed him to the onsite ER section of the hospital.

I sobbed. My mom and older sister, Sheri, were there, but I didn't want to do this without Jason.

The medical staff told me we could wait for Jason, but I confessed to the nurses that I felt the urge to push. They looked at each other nervously.

Then Noah's heart rate got slower. And slower.

Finally, the nurses validated my need. *You gotta push,"* one said.

I pushed. I pushed for Noah, and, now I realize, generations before me. As I pushed, Jason ran into the room. He took my right arm and cheered me on. We both wept when Noah was finally born. The release of a generational curse.

I ended a cycle of a line of women who had been forced to ignore their needs, so they could be everything for their children.

I thought about the strain this placed on their ability to nurture and softly care for their children.

Especially for my mother and grandma, being immigrants from Jamaica. There was a driving pressure to provide the American dream that eclipsed the emotions of their children. Their job as mothers was to provide, keep us alive, and pave the way for our future success.

Our job was to be on our best behavior, perform our roles, and reduce their stress by not asking for more.

Then I saw my uncle, who came through at the conference's breathwork session. His aura was canary yellow. And with it came the energy of both the sacred masculine that can provide support and the nurturing energy of the divine feminine.

Then a wave of guilt crashed over me, because I believed his death was untimely.

After the conference's breathwork session, I told my newfound friend, Jessica, what I had seen. I told her about my uncle's death, and she felt into the energy.

She said it was his karma to pass the way that he did and that it was allowing something to be fulfilled. It wasn't until today that I felt like I truly understood that.

Throughout my family's lineage, there has been a son that provides. My mom and my grandma had my uncle. When my mom divorced my biological father, we moved from Miami to a small town in Tennessee to move in with my uncle.

He embodied financial stability. While my grandma was looking for work in America, so that she could bring my mom and my uncle over, my uncle was saving money, and socking it away even as a small child.

His sense of purpose was to care for others. To be a role model. To show that life can be easy.

Work for him was fun, social, and creative. He was part of running the railroad stations in a small town where he found fulfillment, community, and belonging. He was inspiring to everyone.

He did what he was good at, what he loved, and the Universe blessed him with abundance. So much so that he was able to pay for both of his grandchildren's college tuition.

It immediately took me back to being around seven or so years old when I decided that I was going to be a tomboy, because I wasn't, "pretty." I was at Kmart and it was time for me to pick out new shoes for school. I picked out camo like hiking boots, because I thought that's what masculine was.

At the time, I was doing it out of a fear of rejection, but in the session I realized that it was a calling to heal something within myself and my family. That it was okay to be a strong, masculine, proactive person with a kind, sensitive heart.

I saw my own sons, their effervescent smiles. With their own births, I was reborn. It is an honor to be their mother. And once again, breaking that cycle of birth being a double-edged sword of a burden and a blessing, because of the self-sacrifice it required from my ancestors.

I saw them holding my hands, encouraging me. They were also wrapped in that canary yellow energy. A sign that they are that exact embodiment of the divine feminine and the sacred masculine blended together without any judgment or desire to be something else.

Then the phrase "I am my mother's son" came to my mind. I was living out my uncle's legacy, right here, right now. Helping others to feel supported and showing them that it can be easy, fulfilling, and joyful.

I was being tasked or blessed with this gift to once again bring in a generation of ease, of healing. Where there isn't the trauma of having to sacrifice our well being or parts of ourselves in order for us to live a life where we have what we need, what we want, and beyond.

We can all be providers. We can all be nurturers. We are all a beautiful blend of the divine feminine and the sacred masculine, but it's up to us how we express it. The only limitations on how we show up are self-imposed indoctrinations that we're too afraid to question.

Next came the number 13. Before the breathwork session, I pulled a card from *The Breath of Gold Oracle Deck* we received as a welcome gift. I pulled card number 67, *"Breathe in Manifestation."*

In numerology, you take numbers at face value, but you also add them together. The 6 signifies service, caring for others, and responsibility. The 7 is truth-seeking, spirituality,

At the time, I was doing it out of a fear of rejection, but in the session I realized that it was a calling to heal something within myself and my family. That it was okay to be a strong, masculine, proactive person with a kind, sensitive heart.

I saw my own sons, their effervescent smiles. With their own births, I was reborn. It is an honor to be their mother. And once again, breaking that cycle of birth being a double-edged sword of a burden and a blessing, because of the self-sacrifice it required from my ancestors.

I saw them holding my hands, encouraging me. They were also wrapped in that canary yellow energy. A sign that they are that exact embodiment of the divine feminine and the sacred masculine blended together without any judgment or desire to be something else.

Then the phrase "I am my mother's son" came to my mind. I was living out my uncle's legacy, right here, right now. Helping others to feel supported and showing them that it can be easy, fulfilling, and joyful.

I was being tasked or blessed with this gift to once again bring in a generation of ease, of healing. Where there isn't the trauma of having to sacrifice our well being or parts of ourselves in order for us to live a life where we have what we need, what we want, and beyond.

We can all be providers. We can all be nurturers. We are all a beautiful blend of the divine feminine and the sacred masculine, but it's up to us how we express it. The only limitations on how we show up are self-imposed indoctrinations that we're too afraid to question.

Next came the number 13. Before the breathwork session, I pulled a card from The Breath of Gold Oracle Deck we received as a welcome gift. I pulled card number 67, "Breathe in Manifestation."

In numerology, you take numbers at face value, but you also add them together. The 6 signifies service, caring for others, and responsibility. The 7 is truth-seeking, spirituality, and experimentation. Adding them together leads us to the karmic number, 13.

Thirteen is a number of cycles and transformations—very Plutonian energy. May 2024 was also a 13 Universal month. May, the 5th month plus each individual number in 2024 equals 13. A month of karmic beginnings and endings. There are 13 weeks in each season. It's a lifelong rhythm that we experience. It enables us to shift and clear energy. That was a word that came up also during breathwork: Clear.

Seeing all of these things put together and having this experience of clarity, brought me back to the intention-setting ceremony. I don't need to hold myself back in my business. I need to make things easy for myself, instead of martyring myself for "the benefit of others." My purpose is to not only be a cycle breaker in my family line, but to also to teach other sensitive, intuitive souls how to break cycles as well.

Breaking cycles requires asking for what you want and then having the openness to fully receive it without judging yourself for not having it. That is a chronic issue, especially for women of color and children of immigrants. We feel like we should not need anything.

We should have everything figured out and therefore be needless and always be ready. Always ready to provide for others, regardless of the damage it causes to ourselves.

When we speak up, when we are true to ourselves, we get exactly what we need and even more. We model to our loved ones the ability to be more integrated individuals and less compartmentalized work horses and people-pleasers.

Because money is just an energy, a resource, trusting who you are holistically will bring money to you, because you're in alignment with your purpose, the karmic cycles, and your own unique energy.

Instead of hiding who they are to receive surface-level acceptance, they can show their families a new way of being. This allows them to heal their families through both the material and the spiritual realms by trusting their strengths, honoring their needs, acting on their intuition, and shining light on the dark places of our society, of our culture, of our family.

I was taken back to the conference's breathwork session once more. I saw my five-year-old self. She was very confident, very secure in herself, warm to all, and just happy to be. I was with a friend, and I was leading them through a meditation—not uncommon for me at that age.

I got the message immediately. Our true purpose lies in our childhood.

So what are those things that you used to do that brought you so much joy, that felt like it needed to be expressed through you? Because that is your purpose, your truth, and your path to fulfillment.

May 4th, 2024: Day 2 of the Retreat

In my breathwork session today, I heard *"depth requires darkness."* There was this visual feedback loop of watching myself as a child. I witnessed her desire to be herself, to play with others, and to be understood.

My five-year-old self grabbed my hand, leading me through a field.

She kept saying, *"Let's play! Come on. Let's do the thing that we're made to do!"*

Then I saw my eight-year-old self in the fetal position.

She questioned my five-year-old self, *"Is this okay? If I do this, will I be okay? How do I know I'll be okay?"*

I asked my eight-year-old self, *"Why do you feel that way? What's wrong?"*

And I saw a memory from that time. I called my best friend to wish her a happy birthday.

Her parents answered the phone and said, *"She can't come to the phone. She's having her birthday party right now."* My eight-year-old self was crushed.

A rush of heartache and guilt overwhelmed her. It accompanied the belief that the more authentic I am, and the more that I need, the less lovable I am.

WOOSH. I was taken back to a past life where I was a temple priestess. My job was to serve the community and to lead. And even though I had all that influence and all that power and all that visibility, it was hollow.

I wasn't able to connect with people in a vulnerable space. I wasn't able to have needs, emotional needs. Physical sure, but emotional needs were not permitted. When I couldn't suppress my emotional needs any longer, the head of our order demanded I do a ritual to call in my replacement.

In the ritual, I poisoned myself, so the new priestess could ascend. Because, essentially, I was tainted. I was no longer considered pure. After death, the vision continued. In the afterlife, I was in a crypt, literally chained to all the people who I had served while they were alive. And that was disheartening. It was just almost like proof that I was wrong for needing anything in the first place.

WOOSH. That brought me back to a vision of my first serious relationship at sixteen years old. I saw a mass of darkness. Before, I attributed it to him—his cheating, substance use disorder, and dishonesty. This time, I understood the darkness that he exhibited was a reflection of my own darkness, and that darkness isn't inherently bad.

Darkness is an energy and it is something that you can channel to be something else. How it is channeled through our bodies and what we choose to do with it is always our choice.

Then, a flood of good memories from that relationship washed over me.

I asked my guides, *"What is the purpose of this?"*

They showed me that I was there to show him that he was capable of feeling that depth of love. Because of his mental health struggles, he questioned if it was possible for him.

The feedback loop of longing to be loved and understood felt complete. Yes, I had experienced betrayals and rejection. Yes, it was painful. And yes, it was purposeful.

Yes, there was darkness there from past lives and from this current incarnation, but it was representative of my own self-rejection. He was another part of me.

Then I saw a parade of other male figures who have loved me throughout my life.

My first memory in this lifetime arose. I was in my crib and the spirit of one of my ancestors poked at my cheeks, describing how beautiful and funny and great I was going to be.

My first major crush in elementary school, Patrick. I remember seeing him for the first time. Time slowed, and I heard music. It was an immediate soul connection. We would say "I love you" when we talked on the phone. After we broke up, we were still close. He would even recite my poetry by heart throughout middle school.

Back to Mike. I was taken back to the night of a high school football game where we hugged goodbye. We had broken up months ago. He just gave me a big kiss on the neck and we both said I love you. It was childlike and wholesome. Even when we grew apart and stopped talking as much, he would reach out occasionally to check in. I remember being so confused about that. How could someone love me so deeply without it being conditional?

Earlier that day, all of the retreat participants climbed Cathedral Rock to experience the energy of one of Sedona's most powerful vortexes. At the top, Darren was talking to a kind-spirited man. Hesitantly, I joined in. By the end of the conversation, the man asked to take a selfie of the three of us to remember the moment.

"Bye," I said.

"Bye, Mike," said Darren. I gave Darren a look. I told him about the song in the car and my request that Mike show up differently.

Darren said, "Did you hear what he said to me?" I shook my head. *"I said, 'Nice to meet you.' And he said, 'Nice to see you."*

My heart overflowed with gratitude.

WOOSH. I next was catapulted into seeing my husband, Jason. I was enveloped in the knowing that he is exactly what I needed in this lifetime—stability, kindness, nurturing, strength, resilience, and loyalty. It felt like I was floating on the ocean. I was me, but Jason's presence in my life was the water holding me as the waves rose and fell—the ups and downs of life.

The sensation cemented a new belief within me: it's okay for me to play. It's okay for me to be curious.

It's okay for me to have been all the versions of myself because there is no true identity. I can be anything that I want to be, I don't have to be boxed in. It doesn't make me wrong or inauthentic to explore and evolve. I'm just enjoying the fullness of being a human. And that's what I deserve. I deserve that freedom and the joy that comes with it. In fact, all the joy that I've experienced is my purpose.

Aloud in the session, I burst into laughter. The laughter spread to the other participants. A subtle chuckle among us became a tidal wave of raucous laughter. It was freeing, uplifting, and grounding all at once.

A realization struck me—this is how I lead. I lead by doing. I lead by being. I don't need to be perfect.

My eight-year-old self balked at my behavior.

"How can I be loved if I'm not perfect? If I have needs? Who's going to be willing to fill them?" she questioned.

I felt the energy needing to be released and I asked Adrienne to put her hands on the backside of my heart chakra. She led me into a yogic child's pose position, and once her hands were placed on my back, I felt a release akin to childbirth.

But instead of another human being, I birthed a new version of myself, a new version of my business.

At that moment, the name Aurelia (meaning "the golden one") popped into my head. It was the name Jason and I had decided on for our second child—who we knew would be a girl. (Instead, we were blessed with Ian—exactly whom our family needed.)

The namesake, had we had a girl, was Marcus Aurelius, the Roman emperor, philosopher, and poet. An extremely impactful person. As a society, we view power and influence as something forceful. Something that harms more than it helps. But in reality, it's holding space.

It's trusting yourself. It's allowing yourself to lead the way even if you don't know that you're leading.

I then saw myself leading droves of people over the horizon. I was confident, and I didn't know where I was going. Then fear struck again as I watched myself leading. "Oh, God, what if I lead these people wrong?" The darkness of self-doubt ready to be seen and integrated.

Then, my mind's eye was flooded with the color red. Red is the color of the root chakra. Its mantra is *"I am."* This energy center holds who we are at soul-level.

When I was an actor, I wore red all the time. Emotionally, it made me feel powerful, like the Universe was at my beck and call. It also brought out my sensuality. Psychologically, I knew people who wore red were seen as more attractive—which was always a leg up in an industry based on sexuality and power.

My fiery energy used to scare me. I was told by my first acting coach that I had a presence—when I entered a room, people noticed. Once I realized the true nature of the entertainment industry is to manipulate and puppeteer, I started to hide my fiery energy (part of my sacred sexuality) to avoid being taken advantage of. I disconnected from that part of myself, viewing it solely as destructive.

But fire is also creative.

When we are able to view our *"imperfections"* as untapped skills, we are able to create something magical and otherworldly, because we're not confined by the expectations of society or what the past has brought us.

These untapped skills are useful, they're purposeful, and they exist to change the face of humanity. When we learn how to wield them—like any other tool—we create something new. We are revolutionary in our energy.

My mind drifted back to red and white striations of the mountains we saw from the peak of Cathedral Rock. The red reminded me of the fire of my Leo moon. My Leo Moon really wants to make other people smile, doesn't want to just have the credit for itself, it symbolizes play, lots of joy, and wants everyone to be in on it, and for everyone to have a great experience.

That is how we move forward in this world—by caring about all people. When we're fueled by love and curiosity, we're not afraid to set the standard by trying something new or unexpected. Instead, we can recognize it as the source of our strength and power.

A burst of energy surged within me. I stopped feeling that I have to hide parts of myself because they're unexpected or imperfect. I am me, and my existence is purposeful.

Even when I burn something down, because of the natural energy that I have, that is for a reason. It sparks passion, changes dynamics, and moves emotional energy to burn away inauthenticity.

Yes, fire burns. It devours. But it also precipitates creation. In indigenous cultures worldwide, there is an agricultural practice called Slash and Burn. They purposefully burned land in order to help it grow back more fertile with increased biodiversity. It helped maintain crops, so that the soil wasn't drained of its nutrients.

Destruction is simply another energy that can be used to create a positive impact, a devastating one, and/or everything in between. There's nothing inherently wrong with it outside of what our brains have taught us—we need sameness in order to survive. We've vilified loss and feared change, when, in actuality, we need to let things go for something new and more aligned to come to fruition.

It reminds me of so many powerful humans throughout history. Harriet Tubman. Rupaul Charles. Martin Luther King Jr. Gandhi. They all challenged and destroyed structures and flouted social conventions in order to change the world.

If we want to have fulfilling lives, we have to be willing to (figuratively) burn things down. It might be uncomfortable, it might be uncommon, but it creates a new space for something else to come in. This is paramount for people who are wanting to live a more spiritually aligned life.

In business, be willing to burn down these perceptions of ourselves that other people have, and know that it's not wrong to try something differently, to embody your dream differently. It's just a choice. It's just a form of meditation. It's just play.

And when we make it more than that, we are boxing ourselves in, stifling our energy, and not allowing ourselves the success that we truly desire. Which is being authentic and loving ourselves and inspiring others to do the same.

As if to tie it all up in a bow, I had a sudden remembrance of the night before. I asked my guides, "Okay, what else do I need to know before I go to bed?"

They had me pull a card. It was number 31 from The Breath of Gold Oracle Deck, "Breathe Into Stillness." It was all about letting go of other people's ideas of success and how it's created. The words written in the guidebook said to spend more time creating my version of success and diving into that energy.

May 5th, 2024: Day 3 of the Retreat

On the last day of the retreat, my body demanded integration. I had experienced so much energy moving from the breathwork over the last few days. My belly felt upset and I drank seltzer water and ginger tea to calm the rumbles in my abdomen.

The tea was Yogi brand and it came with a little saying on the tag. It read, *"The breath is the voice of the Spirit."* My stomach settled with the drinks and I was able to relax into the breathwork session.

We did our final breathwork session as a group outside. The wind, the trees, and the frog who watched from the railing grounded my body in a way I didn't expect. It allowed the healing to integrate somatically.

Inside, the vibe had been focused on ethereal, cosmic connections.

Outside, the energy was based in the present—what I needed to do in reality right now in order to manifest the things that I desire in my life.

The first vision I saw was of myself hosting groups for the sake of hosting groups, just because it would be fun. I love people. And I love discovering their soul's blueprint through energy reading and Astrology. It's like solving a puzzle. I feel a thrill helping people better understand and subsequently love and trust themselves.

I saw myself hosting a meetup for women who are spiritually led and want to have a business, and that feels creatively fulfilling and involves a lot of play.

And that brought me back to the idea of a retreat I conceived with a former business partner called the Profit Playground. It was such a delight to envision women realizing that they could attain financial freedom by being themselves and having fun. Instead of neglecting their creative impulses, I would guide them on how to really lean into them and see what they were able to manifest by doing so.

I saw myself in airports around the world, taking pictures at famous landmarks with diverse groups of women, teaching Astrology and intuition. So many retreats.

My body squirmed. I felt myself shying away from the idea of being a leader. In my body, leadership equated to pressure and manifested as an upset stomach.

Now that I was totally tapped into my body, I equated that sensation of pressure with perfectionism. I opened up my body posture, allowing myself to energetically open to the belief that I can lead without being perfect. I can help others without needing to know all the answers for them. I am not here to be someone else's solution or panacea; I'm here to collaborate.

Suddenly, I found myself needing to use the restroom. I asked for help getting up and soon found that my balance was off-kilter. Adrienne kindly walked me to and from the bathroom door.

Afterward, I settled back into the breathwork. Three days ago, needing help to walk to the bathroom would've been humiliating, unacceptable, and burdensome. Now, I felt safe.

Chills rippled through my body. I raised my hand. Adrienne told me to vocalize what I was feeling. Eventually, she coaxed me into using words to describe the bundle of sensations in my body.

"It's okay to need things," I choked out. Before I knew it, I was sobbing uncontrollably. A cleansing release.

It evolved into it's safe to be supported—which can be hard for women to embrace. It had always felt taboo to need those things both in this life, and in the past. It's felt as though if I need something, then I am a problem. I am inherently a burden, and I'm not doing what I'm supposed to be doing.

Physically receiving help, comfort, and sometimes just a hand to hold during the session, embedded the realization that receiving is equal to giving. Neither is better than the other. Neither makes you a good or bad person. In complete alignment with my Libra Sun, it's all about balance and open heartedness.

If we are solely open to giving, we miss out on part of that cosmic cycle of receiving. We miss out on an opportunity to truly connect to one another.

Receiving and giving are part of a divine cycle. They teach us flexibility, openness, adaptability, and presence. You don't need to have all the answers to be valuable. To be worthy. To help people. You just need to show up and assess on a moment by moment basis, and everyone will get exactly what they need in the situation without needing to preempt it.

With that realization, came the heaviness of grief and sadness. This was the transformation I had sensed as I waved goodbye to my family in the backseat of the black SUV.

I didn't need to live these old beliefs fueled by intrusive thoughts and fear of rejection. I was birthing something new.

I started to feel movement in my abdomen. Adrienne held my hand and prompted me to make a primal noise. I yelled from the depths of my soul, from the center of my root chakra. In that moment, I had a vision of seeing myself birthing myself.

I am the child. I am the one who needs to have a sense of safety with being myself, instead of always providing it for others. That responsibility felt challenging, yet comforting. I had seen it countless times before in my own life and others'. When we take good care of ourselves, it creates a powerful ripple effect, benefiting those around us.

This new body-level belief gave me the power that I so deeply wanted, rather than giving it away to another.

I saw my six-year-old son, Noah, in the vision. He expressed how much he believed in me. And how proud of me he was. Noah handed me a purple hibiscus flower. Purple is often associated with the crown chakra, the energy center where we receive intuitive wisdom from the divine. Hibiscus flowers are for cleansing. It felt like a gift of freedom, acceptance, and understanding.

I also saw my three-year-old, Ian. He was urging me to let go and leave room for more of his own independence. I watched him joyfully run around. A reminder that I, too, deserve to live a life of joy and pleasure.

We can create so much just by being. My children show me daily that we are all inherently powerful creators. When we tell ourselves we aren't enough, we aren't worthy, or there's something wrong with us, we strip ourselves of our power.

We ignore and undermine our unique gifts and we feel like wholeness is outside of ourselves. We don't need to be fixed. We need to be us. And love doing it.

I felt complete clarity around my business now. I need to play. I need space to explore. And even if I just gave myself a month of putting myself out there while following my passions, rather than sacrificing them to follow outdated conventional wisdom, success was imminent.

If you're an entrepreneur, don't feel trapped by other people's expectations. You must carve your own path and embrace your individual power and desires—a balance of the sacred masculine and divine feminine.

And you'll find, as all cycle breakers do, that we always have what we need, if we're willing to ask for it.

Erin Kathleen Cummings

In Which She Learns the Word "Conviviality": A Breathwork Story

Saturday, June 15, 2024

I have been invited to participate in writing a multi-authored book about breathwork. I am jazzed. I am feeling pretty damn cool. Adrienne says I always have "epic" journeys, and I figure that must, somehow, reflect well on me. So, perhaps, I enter this opportunity with a little shameless ego. It comes after seven months of nearly non-stop efforts at personal growth and self-improvement. It comes after several plant-medicine healing journeys and a whole lot of breathwork. It comes after a self-induced heartbreak and a slew of tough realizations about my own ability to live in denial and delusion when the truth hurts just a little too much. *"But now,"* I think, *"now, I'm more healed, more whole."* I have it all figured out.

Let the breathwork begin.

Breathwork Journey #1

Sometimes you pull the perfect oracle card just before you go into a breathwork session. In fact, if you believe in that sort of thing, you almost always do. Today I pulled the "Blessed" card from Collette Baron-Reid's Wisdom of the Oracle deck. But I don't have enough time to read the full description of the card and all I see is, *"You feel blessed in ways that are difficult to express. It's as if the Red Sea parts in front of you..."* This reminds me of a favorite Kabbalistic teaching, that before the Red Sea parted for Moses—a blessing delivered unto him and his people by God—he tried to part the sea from the shores and failed. It was not until people began walking into the roiling sea with blind but absolute faith that what would be, would be for the best, that its waters parted and the people were delivered from bondage and into freedom. Swirling around my brain in that flicker of reminder is also an assessment of the Jewish faith by David Brooks in How to Know a Person: For Jews "Life is an audacious moral journey. Life asks a moral question: have you lived up to the covenant?

Have you taken your Exodus journey? Are you striving to be good and repair the world? [Judaism makes] a pressure-packed demand to grow and be better." All this is on my mind in the flash before we lay down to begin the session, all at a time in my life during which I feel strongly I am indeed on my Exodus journey out of a socially and self-imposed bondage and toward my own spirit's liberation. But in so doing, I am walking away from predictable, familiar shores toward a new and unknown sea of possibility, growth, and meeting my soul's purpose.

And that is all before breathwork begins. Oy vey, am I right?

The first thing I remember during the session is Adrienne guiding us to imagine we are somewhere in nature with the sun on our face, and, perhaps a bit unsurprisingly, I find myself on those very shores of the Red Sea. Only, unlike the Ten Commandments movie version, it isn't dramatically dark and stormy. I stand at the shore, staff in hand, my arms spread wide and a smile on my face as the warm sun gently caresses my cheeks. I am Moses and I feel blessed without knowing why, as chaos and desperation swirl around me. I slam down my staff, but...nothing. I slam it down again. No luck. Is God there? I begin to falter, to fear, to reject. *"Why on earth do I think I can part the sea?"* I wonder.

It is not until my people, my beloved people—more courageous, more patient, more faithful than I—begin hurling themselves into the sea that I finally take my first tentative steps forward into the water. And when I do, it finally parts. Gloriously. Magically. Faithfully. Cinematically. It occurs to me, very clearly, that the best answer I can give anyone when they ask me what my next steps are, what purpose I seek in this lifetime, and how I will accomplish my soul's most inspired work here on earth, is *"I don't know."* I just know that I have changed profoundly, that I am walking toward something meaningful and true, and I can't know any more than that without walking myself into that deep unknown. I like to think I'm like a kid who believes they're drowning, only to find that if they calm down and reach out a toe, they can actually touch the bottom. I'll climb out of this water one way or another, but I have to walk in with faith first, faith that whatever happens is for my highest good and the best possible outcome once I do.

Humans will do a lot (or maybe just I will) to not have to surrender to the unknown, to avoid relinquishing even the slightest sense of control over outcomes. Perhaps that is why an intense insecurity and limiting belief comes to me in this moment of my breathwork journey: "You're too ugly to be loved and no one will accept you," it states, matter-of-factly. Ouch, Ego, that was harsh. But, having embraced the "the only way out is through" philosophy lately, I decide to sit with that idea, lean into the feeling of it. "Okay," I say, "I'm ugly." And I cry. Heavily and for a long time. But as I cry woefully at the thought of my own weird and uneven face, my lumpy, rolling body, my stout physique, and my goofy hair that never quite does what I want, I feel hands of love supporting me from below, touching my body with kindness and delivering the clear message that beauty comes from within. At that moment, I simply accept this truth. My ego doesn't even step in—like it is now, in the aftermath as I write—to say that's just something ugly people tell themselves to feel better. If I can tell you something about breathwork right here and right now, it's that some messages are difficult to receive. I regularly resist receiving the message that I am worthy. I know, intellectually and philosophically, that just by virtue of being a glittery little hunk of universal spirit encapsulated in a human skin, I am worthy, but on a deep internal level, I'm fighting my inherent worthiness and perhaps that of everyone else. Either way, you don't come out of one single breathwork session 100% healed of all your woundings. There is work yet to be done.

And so, we persist. The breathwork continues. We are guided to imagine ourselves surrounded by our ancestors. In a way, I am already surrounded. As my awareness lingers on my ugliness, I think disapprovingly of my asymmetrical face, the way one of my eyes gets squintier than the other when I smile or laugh, the way my smile doesn't open up across my face the way I imagine it does, and how photographs of myself are often a disappointment. Suddenly, now, though, I am not me, or at least not me in this lifetime. I am with my ancestors, around a fire, perhaps in one of my former lives. I am an indigenous woman with a perpetual smile upon my face. I am old—older than we expect to live even now—but youthful in my laughing, gleeful spirit. I feel that I am, if not a medicine woman, certainly someone whose love and light heals

63

just as effectively as medicine.

Embodying this deeply lovable woman, I notice that one side of my face—the left side, the feminine side—is always lit up in a joyful smile that crinkles my left eye into a happy crescent moon turned topsy-turvy. But I notice that the right side of my face barely moves at all, either from injury or some little irregularity in my DNA. Either way, it is paralyzed. It is on the left side where my unique way of expression, that my beaming love, is captured in that one joyfully squinty left eye. *"Ah,"* I think very calmly with confident knowingness, *"that's why my eyes are not symmetrical in this life—it's a gift from my past life to remind me that I am joy."* In this vision, I realize that I also have abnormally long arms—but they reach out so lovingly to the souls around me that I simply cannot see them as wrong or ugly in any way. Despite my physical differences, too, the ancestors around me love me, see into my beautiful spirit, and as I embrace several of them, affectionately, I can sense that these are my soul family even today, people whose inner beauty, inner value and worth, I sometimes struggle to honor when I'm being particularly judgmental and puffed up with arrogance. But what I understand now, during this episode of this one breathwork journey, is something quite significant: if I judge myself for my imperfections, it follows that I will judge others for theirs. The work is within.

The last message I remember receiving during this breathwork journey is that I must release the need for external validation.

If there's another thing I can say about breathwork, it's that breathwork doesn't happen in a vacuum. At this particular moment, I happen to be reading Sonia Choquette's Ask Your Guides, and this evening I decide it's time to speak with whom she calls my "teacher guides." I voice-record the session in case I connect with them, not expecting much success. What happens is what I can only describe as full-blown channeling.

They tell me, among other things, and verbatim:

(1) You need to learn more about self-love. Because it's the key to sharing your love with others through healing work. You don't have to be perfect, but a little bit more will go a long way.

(2) You need to learn to see without judgment. See others in all of their beauty, embrace them with compassion, hold them in your heart, without judgment. Right now you're judging everyone and you gotta stop that. You're a good girl, but you know better.

(3) Keep learning. Take all the opportunities that you can afford. And you can afford a lot.

(4) Follow your heart. Your heart is your compass.

(5) You're hiding from the truth. The truth of your calling. You are afraid of it because you don't think that you are enough. You're hiding from sadness from long, long ago. Addressing it will heal you and make you more confident and even more joyful. It's sadness from another life. It's sadness from this life. It's sadness you feel some days here, now. It's loss. It's hope. It's disappointment. You were a queen and you lost everything.

(6) The work ahead of you is noble, worthy, and needed. Just be yourself, and your impact will ripple out from the center like a raindrop hitting water. Don't fear this.

What a day...

Sunday, June 16, 2024

I return for a second morning of breathwork at Adrienne's virtual breathwork retreat. It is gentle and kind. My mind, my heart, my spirit, my guides—they all know somehow that today I just need to be nurtured.

As soon as we begin our second breathwork journey of the weekend, led by Adrienne, we are instructed to see our higher selves. When I see my higher self, she is receptive and surrendered. She takes the shape, despite my Jewishness, of Mother Mary (who, let's get real, was also a pretty formidable Jewish mother), her head bowed, hands open, all serenity and peace and love. The only thing different about her from the traditional depiction of Mary is that she is made of the universe. She is a night sky full of stars and space-sparkles and little galaxies glowing with life. She often holds me in the palm of her hand. I am so small in comparison. What will it take to grow to her size and shape, to her exact likeness? When will I be an effervescent being made of stars? Or am I already?

Lately, I have been plagued by the fear of being seen, and breathwork made that abundantly clear today as I was instructed by my loving guides to release that fear of being seen. It is the only way to become who I am supposed to be. *"Let yourself be seen,"* my guides repeat over and over, so compassionately, so gently, so profoundly. But what does it mean to be seen? How can I allow myself to be seen when I can barely see myself? The truth is, I'm still uncomfortable with this woman that I'm becoming. She is serious. She is wiser than ever. She is compassionate. She embodies peace as never before, more skilled at regulating her nervous system. She is intuitive. She connects and speaks with and channels her guides and is capable of sensing their presence all around her and inside her heart every day. In fact, in breathwork today it was her guides who were giving her all that soft, tender care. But why, why is she so uncomfortable in this new skin? Why does she feel separate from it? Why does she feel so...ashamed? Perhaps it's because she has chosen to step into a more potently authentic version of herself and realizes now that she'd not been honoring her truest self for many years. It's a shame she will have to overcome through self-forgiveness and deep, abiding self-love.

Monday, July 15, 2024

Integration

It's taken a month to understand the lessons of the breathwork journeys described above. It usually takes me some time to comprehend the deeper messages and lessons of my journeys and to integrate them into my everyday life. Sometimes I rack my brain for answers, but I find it much more fruitful, to receive the wisdom meant for me with stillness and humility, trusting that the answers will come how and when they do. Breathwork is a tool of the work, and there's just no rushing it. So, I waited quietly, though somewhat impatiently, until this arrived in my heart, another channeled gift from my guides: Protection is power. Protect your peace. Protect your dreams. Protect your home. Protecting your life from people who are still living rooted in fear is essential. The old woman had no fear. She was authentic.

She was warm. She was willing to extend herself, her soul, her spirit to the people around her unabashedly and with equanimity. If someone had told her to fear loving fearlessly, to fear giving generously, to fear the call of her spirit, she would have been a very different woman. Her alignment would have been at stake. It takes courage like Moses to step into your essence. The sea is a fearful, churning obstacle in that allegory, in that story. Fear is the obstacle to freedom, and it is only your steps, fully faithful, fully surrendered, fully trusting that you have everything you need to move forward that miraculously and powerfully and catastrophically sends fear, repels fear, from you. Fear can't stand to be around faith. Fear flees from faith. And some fear is good, some fears protect us, but in this case, fear is to be avoided. Stay true. Stay exquisite. Live in love and surrender. Live as if constantly supported by a unanimous, "Yes." Tinker with life, and play its little games. Be in amusement always with life. Keep yourself amused. The word amused itself suggests muses are all around us—life is the muse. Doing what we love and what brings us joy and contentment and peace is the muse that inspires a life well-lived. Amusement is a trivial word in its current connotation, but to be in amusement is to be in a state of constant inspiration, exhilaration, and conviviality with Source. To live in amusement is oneness and wholeness and unity. Living in amusement gives you the twinkle that you see in the night sky. You're a twinkly little speck of dust, and that's an amusing speck of dust to be.

There really isn't a word in the English language to capture what we're all meant for, but we are all meant for inclination. Picture a hill, an incline, the shaley top of a mountain peak. The easy way about this incline is down—the way of gravity—or you can choose the hard way, which is to climb up it. To be living in inclination is to make the easiest choice, and the easiest choice is always the one of ease, of course, and alignment. If you laid your body perpendicular to the incline, you wouldn't be able to stop yourself from rolling down, so don't stop yourself from the ease of rolling down, even if it frightens you. Why do we choose to climb when our path is so clearly what it is meant to be by way of inclination, when we could just lie down and slide into our purpose and destiny? We must stop making things so hard.

Sometimes you pull the perfect oracle card just before you sit down to complete your chapter of a multi-authored breathwork story. In fact, if you believe in that sort of thing, you almost always do. After channeling, with overwhelming gratitude, the bountiful messages above, I pulled the *"Crow Spirit"* card from Collette Baron-Reid's Spirit Animal Oracle. It reminds me, how "magic pulses through the world," how "every thought can become a thing." It also assures me: "...you are right on target now to see your dreams magically come into being... Remember to be grateful and praise what is yours, even if it is still coalescing into form, still residing in the invisible realms of co-creation..."

All this is to say that when I live in alignment with what and who I am, when I behave and act from a place of authenticity, of amusement, and of trust in a loving universe, I am in inclination. I am on the right, easeful path, the breeze fluttering my hair ecstatically as I flow, down, down, into a life well-lived. Amen.

Rachel Gossett

Freeing Myself from Thirty-Three Years of Eating Disorders

I vividly remember one day in seventh grade, I sat down to a picture with harsh words scribbled on my desk. *"You are so fat. So ugly. And you will never have a boyfriend."* I remember erasing the words on my desk hoping that no one else would see them.

The daily bullying continued throughout the seventh and eighth grade. I never told anyone, not even my parents. I didn't feel safe sharing with my family. My father was extremely critical of EVERYTHING I did. My mother was going through her own mental health issues and eating disorders. I also did not share because I felt an incredible amount of shame and guilt for being me. I was not good enough for my family or society.

Over the last thirty-three years, it has been a roller coaster ride struggling with body dysmorphia, anorexia, bulimia, and binge eating. I tried a variety of traditional modalities such as treatments and recommendations from psychiatrists and psychotherapists. The traditional ways were not enough for me. I didn't know where to turn or who to go to, so I just dealt with it by myself.

In 2015, I was introduced to holistic modalities and complementary tools such as reiki, mindfulness activities, meditation, yoga, and somatic movement because of severe anxiety and panic attacks. These holistic modalities started to shift my perspectives on life and helped me tremendously with my overall wellbeing. But I continued to have relapses with eating disorders and body dysmorphia.

Because I wanted to be a positive example for my four children, I came to the realization in 2023 I needed to heal from my eating disorders instead of just dealing with them. I yearned for a healthy mindset around food. I found a holistic mentor who I worked closely with for three months. We began to peel back the layers that needed healing within me. During our time together, she introduced me to breathwork. It was transformational. I released an energetic block from my heart center regarding a traumatic experience. The incident and person no longer had a hold on me. I was not triggered anymore. My thoughts and emotions completely shifted in a positive way.

After my breathwork experience, I devoured numerous books about breath and sought for an expert in this field. I stumbled upon Adrienne's website, Breath of Gold, thanks to an internet search. I immediately resonated with her story and all that she had to offer. I signed up for The Breath of Gold Facilitator Program because I strongly believed in her and breathwork as a healing modality. I also started attending her weekly breathwork sessions. I wanted to use breathwork as a way to understand the root cause of my eating disorders and body dysmorphia so I could heal this part of me.

On June 16, 2024, as Adrienne guided me during a circular-connected breathwork session, I set the intention to understand why I have eating disorders and body dysmorphia. What I saw in my mind's eye was so vivid. I saw a shovel in my mind's eye and knew I was ready to dig deep. My body started moving to the beat of the music. My movements were so fluid. The dance began to tell a story of a magical ending. My story of releasing traumatic experiences that no longer served me or my highest good. As with most of my breathwork and meditation practices, I usually see myself dancing. I always wanted to be a dancer who specialized in contemporary dance. I wanted to tell stories with movement. I never pursued being a dancer because I was often criticized for my Puerto Rican curves and body shape.

As I continued to dance, a unicorn and rainbow appeared, before transitioning to a scene of a young child. I didn't know who this boy was, but he felt familiar as if I was him in another time. He was alone because his family passed away. This boy was skin and bones, barely able to walk due to fatigue and malnourishment. He was walking with a small plate of food in the cold rain. It was so cold, my body started to shiver as if I was there with him. The plate of food was knocked out of his hands and something derogatory was said to this boy. I continued to witness scenes of him getting whipped in the back, hiding, and helping others.

As this breathwork session continued, I witnessed several scenes from childhood. I was a little girl and my father smacked me across my face. He was so incredibly angry with me. I did not know what I did wrong. I could feel the sting and burn from the slap on my cheek. I stood there crying as he continued to yell at me. I could not make out what he was saying to me. In the next scene, I was still a little girl but this time he had his hands around my neck. He kept telling me I was good for nothing. That transitioned into my father speaking cruel words to my mother, pulling her hair, and then pushing her down to the floor. Then I saw my father making out with another woman. More memories continued to surface. Now he was drunk and angry. My mother grabbed me and was trying to protect me. She was yelling at him to leave me alone. To leave us alone. This scene moved on to a time when my father squeezed my head so hard and picked me up by my head because I did something wrong. I do not remember the reason why. My mother then became the focus of the childhood memories. She often told me I was overweight and fat. Criticized how clothes fit me or what I was eating.

I vaguely remember some of the scenes I witnessed during breathwork were memories I have not thought about for a long time. These scenes also triggered other memories of the physical and verbal abuse I endured as a child. Everything I did was not good enough, especially in my father's eyes. I remember him scolding me for making a peanut butter and jelly sandwich the wrong way. My childhood experiences shaped me into thinking I was unworthy, needed to please others, seek outside validation, and to mask my authenticity. I would not allow myself to be vulnerable.

After the childhood memories stopped, I heard and saw a garnet crystal. I was urged to use garnet for emotional healing. Around this time, a song on the breathwork playlist focused on trust. A part of the lyrics said, "I trusted in you but you let me down." This hit really hard because I trusted in my parents but they were not emotionally present or mature for me.

As the breathwork session progressed, I felt the energy in my throat chakra. Energy was swirling above me and it felt heavy. My body became uncomfortable. My skin was crawling. I had a sense of urgency to escape and disappear. I was wriggling on the floor. As I was moving, I started rubbing my hands along my body. It felt as if I was rubbing something away. I had to get it off of me. I then quickly brought my hands to my face. It felt like an automatic response to protect myself. An intense wave of emotions stirred inside. Tears began to flood out of my eyes. I was sobbing uncontrollably. I was releasing energetic blocks.

During the crying, visions quickly passed in my mind's eye. I saw the little boy again and heard the word "scarcity." Images of my seven-year-old self being fat shamed by my mother because she had a deep desire to change me so I would be liked and loved. Each of these visions were so vivid, as if I was transported back to witness them in real-time.

I started dancing again. This time, my story focused on my four pregnancies. I was standing in front of a mirror dancing and admiring my baby bump. I felt a huge sense of gratitude for my body. My body was able to create these miracles of life and birth my four children.

I heard Adrienne's voice come in as all of this was unfolding before my eyes and she said, "What is it that you are hoping for in life?" My hope was for my three daughters and son to grow up loving everything about themselves. To speak their truths and be comfortable with who they are. To not shy away and feel like they need to change to fit in. For my children to express themselves freely.

During the final song when we returned to our natural breath, my body felt as if it could not take anymore. My body needed to shut down and rest. That is when I fell asleep.

On June 30, 2024, I participated in another breathwork session facilitated by Adrienne. This time, my intention was to release the eating disorders and body dysmorphia that has haunted me for most of my life.

As the music started on this breathwork journey, I immediately saw myself dancing to the music. My body moved gracefully. The movement was with purpose, with intention. I was telling a story. It said, *"This is my story and I want you to hear it."*

I was then transported into an enchanted forest. There I danced all around, without care. The forest had this golden glow to it. I was surrounded by twinkling fairies. The trees were strong and wise. The trees were whispering words of wisdom to me. Gorgeous flowers bloomed all along the forest floor. Everything embodied a sense of purity. The scene was magical. Then I heard a message, *"You are magic."* I repeated to myself, *"I am magic."*

The scene quickly turned to complete darkness. I was standing off to the left. To the right of me a black vortex materialized. My father appeared standing next to me. In an instant, he was then lifted off the ground and cartwheeled throughout the air straight into the vortex. He was gone. Now my mother appeared and the same incident occurred with her. She was lifted off the ground, cartwheeled throughout the air and straight into the vortex. When she disappeared, I noticed there was a string attached to me. I was tethered to my parents. I did not enter the vortex, but my mother and father still had a hold on me. At some point throughout the breathwork journey, the cord was cut. I felt energy leave my body and knew I was finally free of my mother and father. Free of the conditioning they bestowed upon me. Free of the unworthiness, shame, and guilt I felt for being me.

My body experienced a variety of physical sensations. My whole being was burning, inside and out. My skin felt as if it was on fire. Then I saw my skin burning off my body. After the burning ceased, my whole self was absorbed into the earth. I was buried deep into the earth. Planted for a rebirth.

In this breathwork session, Adrienne led us to a primal scream during the climax. After releasing a scream, my body began to shiver. I felt frozen. A part of me died in the moment. A bright white light appeared. I soon saw myself lying there on my basement floor as I hovered over myself. I was having an out-of-body experience.

Adrienne then prompted us to imagine hugging someone in that moment. I saw my son. He provided me with unconditional love, empathy, and compassion as we hugged. I felt so safe in his warm arms. A deep soul connection existed with him. We were one.

After we released our hug, I started having flashbacks again of childhood. My parents fat shaming me because of the clothes I was wearing. My mother and father sounded like a broken record telling me I did not look right, my clothes were too tight, and I was overweight. I was then brought to my eight-year-old self. This was around the time I started developing. I was bullied because I was curvy and I looked different from the other girls.

Adrienne provided the participants with another prompt, which led me yearning for a hug from my father. I wished he loved me just the way I was, and the way I am today. He is still very critical of me. I needed a father then and I need one now. A protector. A supporter. To be the apple of his eye. Daddy's little girl. Instead, I was everything he did not want me to be. I was not good enough. Criticized every waking moment in my life. I began to sob as I felt these intense emotions arise within me.

The scene changed. I was dancing around a bonfire with the native Taínos of Puerto Rico. From studying my ancestry, I know the Taínos run in my blood. As we danced together, they told me to embrace my curves. To feel my curves. Let my curves move me. Flaunt my curves, which are a part of my heritage. I did as they said. I started dancing seductively and felt unconditional love for myself. The beat of the music was pulsating throughout my mind, body, and soul. I felt so sexy. I do not know if I ever felt like this in my own skin. I mean EVER. To experience this feeling brought pure joy to me. It took me until the age of forty-four to realize my mind, body, and spirit was sexy and beautiful in ways I never thought imagined. It's unbelievable how the conditioning of my parents and society significantly impacted my self-worth and body image.

This breathwork experience comforted me. I came to the realization I needed to embrace being seen. I am not for everyone and that is okay. Embracing my uniqueness will support me to stand in my power. To step into my light. To surrender to the ebbs and flow of life.

As with any meditation or breathwork practice, I received validations and guidance through symbols. In this practice, I saw a gorilla, a puma, and a Care Bear with a rainbow on her belly.

The gorilla represented leadership, authority, compassion, kindness, generosity, honor, thoughtfulness, and resiliency. The puma represented strength, wisdom, intelligence, inner power, confident-self, psychic, ferocity, freedom, instinct, and intuitiveness. The Care Bear with the rainbow belly was one of my favorite characters during childhood. When I saw this Care Bear, it represented giving care to others, healing others, my life's purpose, and helping people to heal their inner child.

After the climax of the session, I felt energy pulsating throughout my body and all around me. It was strong and powerful, like a force field. I envisioned becoming unstoppable at that moment. No one and nothing was going to impact my energy system. I was releasing everything that did not serve me with love and grace back into the earth.

I saw my healing career take a turn. A football whizzed by my head. Men surrounded me as they played. I was then flying through the air and landed at a professional training facility. I entered an office space. The large team logo loomed in front of me. I began working intimately with the large organization and many others to increase their overall well-being, reduce their stress, anxiety, and feeling overwhelmed, to speed up recovery, to increase their growth mindset, and to heal their inner child. I created a heart-centered, safe, calming space for them to release energetic blocks and stagnant energy, and promote restoration of the mind, body, and spirit so they could find relief within.

This session was intense and I fell asleep during the final song. I woke up when Adrienne said to roll over. I was deeply impacted by this practice. I felt like a little child as I remained curled up in the fetal position. I just wanted to sleep it off.

An hour after the breathwork session, my energy was incredibly lighter. The heaviness lifted. I was free. I was on top of a mountain twirling like Julie Andrews and singing the opening song from the Sound of Music. I had this vision once before when I healed from a different past trauma.

Wait a second. Did I just heal from my eating disorders and body dysmorphia in two breathwork sessions? It sure feels that way. I was prompted by Spirit to do automatic writing.

Below is what I received:

Now is the time to shine. This is exactly what you needed. This is why you were feeling stuck. It was because of how you viewed yourself. Now you view yourself with authority. With purpose. You are driven and your goals are achievable because you are deserving. You were never lacking. Your mindset was conditioned to feel this lack. This emptiness of not being enough. So you had to hide. You had to control something. Controlling what you ate and how you looked made you feel like you had a purpose. But that was not your purpose. Your purpose is to heal people. You are such a bright light, Rachel. You shine your light onto others. You create this ripple effect that you need to be more aware of. You impact so many people's lives just with your radiant smile. See that. Look into the mirror and see the light being that you are. You are attractive because of this.

At the time of writing this, it is now three weeks since one of the deepest, most powerful healing breathwork sessions of my life. I continue to feel lighter and different. I look at myself in the mirror and see beauty inside and out. I no longer see a distorted body image. My mind does not ruminate on food. I am showing myself daily self-compassion because I am worthy. I always thought the eating disorders and body dysmorphia would haunt me until my last breath. Because of breathwork and the space Adrienne created, I have healed this part of me. I am so incredibly grateful for her and my experiences. Now, I can fully step into my light.

As I close this chapter, tears fill my eyes, a reflection of the profound transformation I never thought possible. In my darkest moments, I could have never imagined healing from the suffocating grip of my eating disorders. It felt as though I was constantly gasping for air, trapped in a relentless chokehold, each breath a desperate attempt to survive another day in a body that felt like a battleground.

But then, I found breathwork. Through each conscious inhale and exhale, I began to release the deep-rooted pain and heartache that had anchored me to trauma for the past thirty-three years. My breath became my lifeline, an unwavering guide that helped me shed layers of toxic energy buried in the deepest parts of my soul. Each breath carried me closer to safety, closer to myself. It wrapped me in a tenderness I had yearned for my entire life, a self-compassion that finally allowed me to breathe freely.

I became a breathwork facilitator because I want others to experience the same liberation. I want to help those who feel like they're drowning in their own lives, who are suffocated by the weight of their struggles. I want to guide people to rediscover the innate power that resides within their breath, and within themselves. I want them to reclaim their authenticity, to feel the brilliance of their own light so they can share it with the world.

True healing is possible, one breath at a time. Let's walk this path together, inhaling life, exhaling what no longer serves us.

Terese Katz

Layers of Deep Family Healing

It is Mother's Day, 9 p.m. I lie under covers, moonlight sifts in. The pandemic has us sequestered, but I'm cozy here. I'm settling in to start my first conscious connected breathwork journey in a long, long time. I met this practice decades ago, and now I've rediscovered it through meeting Adrienne Rivera, founder of Breath of Gold, potent and right on time.

Guided to relax even more, I feel a vague anxiety about what will happen, if I'll do it right—all that—which soon dissolves. Invited to begin the circular breath, I start to find a rhythm. My heart immediately swells with sadness, tears rise. Soon enough I'll recognize this phenomenon—as my planning-scoping-doing mind recedes, sadness usually swells, wherever the journey to come will take me. For what I don't nurture enough? For the burdens of losses? All that, probably more.

My intention tonight had been to ease the burden of those losses, so many squeezed together in this weird time. To move forward in the best way through knots of tension and uncertainty.

Worries disappear as the breath starts "breathing me"—truly a secret miracle. I don't will it, and I don't even remember my guide's prompting words... but the image arises clear and real: my mother and father, sitting on a couch in my aunt's living room. My mother grew up in this house; my sister, cousins and I played there. The image resembles a photo I own, though parts differ... except for my mother's face. That's the face and frozen smile from the photo.

My mother had died, unwell, on the cusp of this pandemic, not from the virus. By then, I'd realized that she'd done her best, though she'd been a hard person to have as a mother. As a therapist, and as a person who'd been in therapy over the years, I truly understood this and had long stopped fighting it. Now though...this scene. With it came a deep convulsive sadness—and an absolute certainty, felt right in my body, almost as if I were sharing consciousness with her, that my mother just couldn't, couldn't, take care of babies, then children who grew.

I felt her youth and immaturity and helplessness, how she felt no options in life but to be pretty and to smile always and be pleasing always. To hide any darkness. Nothing remained of her to venture out to others, to the world. I felt that now... I more than knew it, I felt it.

In this picture, my father sits static, unhelpful, but I know deep within myself that they both love me, my sister and me, despite their incapacity to be adults taking care of children. It feels like I sob for a long time. I begin to see a distant glimmer of a tribal fire burning, and a sense of being a woman in that clearing, pointing her face at the moon, feeling peace, other women upholding her.

My body settles into a soft relaxation. I feel like all of this knowing has woven into me. It stays.

The pandemic lasted months, then another year, passing with more shocks and upsets. I commit myself to breathwork once a week, and then to learning how to guide others. The regular practice reveals to me more, and then more. I see that this is how it works.

Many spiritual traditions, and some schools of thought in psychology, too, assume that we carry wisdom within that can heal and guide us. An impulse toward health, a "healing intelligence," an inner knowing. "The Timeless Universe Manifesting Through You." Universal consciousness. The collective unconscious. The source of this might be understood, then, as our subconscious mind, or as archetypical memories, or as our inner connection to the divine. Other beliefs and explanations, varying by time and tradition and culture, exist as well. I believe they all hold some facet of truth.

With breathwork, I've found that we can move quickly to this inner source. (In this way, breathwork fully overlaps with psychedelic therapies.) I've found, too, that as we access these images, feelings, and memories, with breathwork also can come a simultaneous knowing that we can hold these. That we are not without strength, or alone. We can know what we need, now or next, as a result.

Breathwork, in a single journey, or as a practice over time, unfolds as this intelligence leads the way. Therefore, what arises might surprise you, or prove relevant in ways you couldn't have predicted. And in an ongoing practice, you might find yourself moving through progressive layers of knowing and arising.

In my own ongoing practice, the layers of family and ancestors showed themselves first. Over weeks, in a thread that became more and more familiar, I grew a sense of how I connected to family, alive and no longer. I remember one journey, months after that Mother's Day. That morning, a deep rage I'd never suspected emerged with images of my father and his verbal meanness. He'd left relatively early on, and died relatively young. I'd carried him as an unfortunate fact and spoke about him with a certain amount of eye-rolling and annoyance. This fury, I'd never met before. My body wanted to punch and kick and scream, "How dare you! How dare you!" In later weeks, he'd appear often in my breathwork as someone whose energy I wanted to fiercely will back down into the core of the earth. "Go away, decompose, leave this sphere."

It didn't arise as one big revelation, but some months after these experiences, I began to notice glimmers of a different awareness: that he wants good for me. Huh. Wherever he is, that he admires me. That he has regrets. That he'd help me as he could. Where this comes from…again, various ways of understanding these kinds of perceptions exist. And again, I find they all reflect something important. In the end, though, it doesn't matter. Really, it's only how I perceive and experience this that matters at all.

After my mother died, among the compounded losses, my sister, my aunt, and my uncle died as well. I'd often wondered why I landed with my mother instead of her older sister, a much more capable person with a lot of traits like mine. I broke down driving home from her memorial. After this, in more than one breathwork session, I began to envision and sense how we all fit together, us change-the-world, keep-everybody-going women of our line, and those more helpless or sidelined.

In other journeys, I not only felt a deep grief and longing for my sister, but I also sometimes felt deep sadness over my inability, as the older girl, to be more consistently kind when we were growing up. We were twenty-two months apart, but I began to see her in my mind's eye as present even as I was being born, on board to come next, her energy already touching mine. I can sometimes see or feel her giving me a tough piece of advice now. Our consciousness still mingled.

So, I still can feel acutely that the family I grew up with is gone. But I now know, effortlessly, that they exist within me. It is a human sorrow but not a horrible tragedy, in the grand flux of things.

Family, ancestors, more unfold as months become a year, and then a second year. I find my way with some repeated images, senses, words—from my own emotional memory banks, from other lifetimes? Again, layers of knowing and unknowing, and I deepen this comfort with the world the breath acquaints me with. I continue to strengthen a sense of who I am and have been over time, what my consciousness has known and brings to my life and work now.

Lately, I seek clarity and strength with the next steps in my life. Life keeps moving, as it does, and crisis years recede. Breathwork keeps moving, too. I follow its flow, notice trends over time.

A recent Sunday: Father's Day. My father doesn't feel present in today's breathwork. This is fine: I feel nothing unresolved there, and the breath doesn't bring me there today. When I start now, I no longer feel anxious. The sadness still swells. Today, I experience a sense of flow, of motion as if in water. I see myself washed through by a waterfall's thunder. The light glistens. I move then to that tribal fire I've come to know. I am anointed by other women there and know I exist in connections moving forward and backward in time's web. I keep asking what's next, what do I need to know, to say, to do... The words and the feeling these days arise with certainty: there is nothing to do. Learn ease. Let it come. You've done a lot of work. Let it settle. See where it takes you.

This is how recent weeks of breath have flowed. Calm, not so dramatic. Easy. I've journeyed a lot. So let it settle for now.

The day after this Father's Day, I rediscovered Matt Kahn's mantra, "When I am feeling _____, I deserve more love, not less". "When he is _____, he deserves more love, not less". "When they _____, they deserve more love, not less". Etc. It lands just right; I am very clear for days.

Today: breathwork one week later. A little anxiety, a little sadness. They dissipate. Starting slowly, I see my father's face, as firm and supportive as he ever could have been. My sister's face lines up just behind. She resembles him. She's always kept a wall there, and now isn't different. As the pace quickens, I then shift to a familiar setting, part of my own inner make-up, I've come to know. A clearing in a rainforest, thick and jungly. That fire circle blazing.

From there, I'm that self, or that inner image, lying in a stream. Face, down, hurt. This echoes a now-familiar scene I've also met in these years. An abbess, somewhere in Europe, massacred, ravaged, in a rocky stream. She could not save the women burned on stakes, nor her daughter. A strong set of "witch wounds", yes. Another layer I've digested over time, sensed changes, unfolding, integrating.

Now, today's scene is a new one. In this stream, it's even earlier, I'm sure. Hooves and shielded men tear off. A jaguar has descended on my body. She's lit a terror in them.

Maybe I continue working this wound much later in time and very far away. Now, in this place, women again anoint me, cool water, oil on my forehead gazing up, their hands beneath me.

I am so grateful for having crossed paths with Adrienne Rivera and rediscovered breathwork.

Through this, I have moved through levels of healing and connection that run deeper than I could have imagined.

After the events shared here, I came to know that I wanted to bring these ways of experiencing to my work with clients. I've been a psychologist for over thirty years. I became a psychologist in part because I was so drawn to understanding what makes us human, how we change and heal and grow. I consider myself a lifetime explorer here. Breathwork seemed an incredibly powerful way of bringing body, mind, and emotion together with higher consciousness and our "innate healing intelligence". A potential means of transformation.

Ultimately, I returned to Adrienne for training to become a certified breathwork facilitator. I'd delved into other training programs and related practices in my research. I found no one more gifted as a breathwork facilitator and teacher. Also, the Breath of Gold certification course is comprehensive in a way that I knew would build my confidence and strength as a facilitator, adding these abilities—and these ways of seeing and understanding—to both therapy and breathwork practice. It continues to be a deeply enriching addition.

We've all been learning, therapists and everyone else, that true healing and change involves our bodily, somatically-held memories. And that it also ideally involves feeling our connectedness to something greater (higher or universal consciousness is one way to name it). My breathwork training has led me to learn more about non-drug avenues to "psychedelic" experiences generally. This ongoing learning energizes me, and I know heightens the quality of my work. I find breathwork to be the best of these modalities.

Since graduating, I've led a woman in breathwork who, for the first time, connected her decades-long body image problems with unwanted sexual experiences she'd dismissed and forgotten. This allowed rapid shifts and changes and a new freedom in her life. I've led another who realized how much breath-holding she does, throughout every day, and has since been able to speak up much more assertively and effectively in her work.

There's a way that the connections made, and feelings that arise, while in breathwork can feel safe and manageable, as we're at the same time connected with inner resources we may have never met before.

Breathwork allows access to heart and spirit in ways that therapy can't always access, or at least not as immediately. As a powerful transformational tool, it requires deep training and space holding. I found that Adrienne thoroughly "gets it" when it comes to teaching the trauma-informed aspect of the certification. This mattered a lot to me. I'm so grateful that I remembered the power of breathwork for myself and my own life, and that now I can support others to find the power of their breath as well.

Kara Stoltenberg

Conversations with My Soul

Looking around the house, I felt confused. It was an unfamiliar space, yet curiosity was my guide as I walked through each room. I was looking for someone. It felt like someone else should be there. As I wandered through the rooms, I noticed the floor was dirt, as if it were an unfinished house. It was night time, but I could see just enough to make my way through the dark, as if there was ambient moonlight and my eyes had adjusted to the darkness of the night. I made my way through the entire house but found no one. It didn't seem right. The emptiness was tangible. I could hear and feel the silence. I was definitely alone. I stopped moving through the rooms and stood still. I felt lost.

It was then that I heard a voice clearly say, *"You have to choose."*

"Choose?" I'm not sure if I thought it or said it.

"Yes. You have to choose. You can go back or you can be done, but you have to make the choice."

It was at that moment that I became aware of a part of me tucked into the fetal position in the corner of the room. She was crying softly. "I can't. I can't do it anymore. I don't have anything left. I can't keep fighting."

But the greater part of me determinedly spoke back to her, "We have to. We're not done. There is more for us to do. We can do this. We're doing this." And just like that, I made my choice. I went back into my body, back into consciousness, back to live my life.

Or so I thought....

"Are you ok?" I kept hearing her unfamiliar voice.

"What happened?" I was so confused. Thinking felt impossible through the fog of my brain.

"You were in a bike accident. We called the ambulance. They're on their way. Is there anyone we can call?" the voice responded.

"My son. I don't know where he is." He was all I could remember and I was all he had. Where was he? I couldn't think. Nothing made sense. I couldn't figure out where I was, why I was here, what day it was, or where Coleman was. Everything was a blur. And yet, the moments are tangibly burned in my memory forever. I didn't know at the time that these were the moments of my new life, in my new body, with my new brain. I didn't know that nothing would ever be the same. I didn't know that at times I would wonder if it would have been better for me to choose to fade into the darkness of that room instead of choosing to come back to my body.

For the six years following the hit-and-run bicycle accident that nearly took my life and left me with a very broken body and a brain injury, I engaged in healing every aspect of my being.

Rebuilding my life, my body and my business brought many healing modalities into my world. Some of my favorite and most profound healing moments came to me through breathwork. In my first six months of consistently doing breathwork with Adrienne in her online breathwork membership, I was invited into one of these moments while on a breathwork journey.

Six months earlier, I had launched Stepping In with Kara, my podcast holding space for other people's stories. As I kicked off Season 2, I decided it was time to tell parts of my story. I did that through conversations with people who had been significant on my journey. On the morning of this breathwork session, as I re-listened to the conversation with my big sister, the message I held in my heart was, "Here is where I am. This is where I am, this is the only place I can be and I have to grow from right here."

I felt so open coming into this breathwork session and held my intention to be fully present, right here... open-hearted to all that is for me right here in my life and in my business. As the journey started off, I was speaking aloud about how sharing my own story freed me to realize in my body that it is no longer about trying to get where I was or trying to get to any future version of me. It is really just about being all of me, right here, growing into the newness of all I will become. ALL OF ME, right here. Loving life, loving my people, creating and being from here.

In breathwork, there is this beautiful space to just be. To have a conversation with your body and receive specific guidance from your higher self, from all that is. The intention you set is very important and, in my experience, it directs and guides what opens during the session. Then again, I feel no pressure as I set my intention because I know I can trust the session to be whatever I need in the moment I am in. The breath can be trusted. For me, it always invites a conversation with my soul. The breath takes me out of my body into a higher state of being and it is easier to access my higher truth and guidance. I get very clear messages that I need to embody and embrace. Sometimes profound healing or emotional release flows through. There is always this beautiful weaving of what Adrienne is saying and the music she is playing as it meets my own voice and what is flowing through me. It is co-creating at its best.

On this day, I had some pain in my body and I kept repeating aloud, "Show me what it is I need to see for healing. Show me what I need to let go."

Eventually, the answer flowed through my voice. *"I have been afraid to just be me, be where I am, and let people see me here. I'm afraid to be honest and believe that the people who are for me will stay with me, even as I am here."* I felt so much emotion acknowledging all the voices that hold me back and keep me where I am "trained" to stay.

I spoke back to them, declaring,

"I have pure courage to step forward into all I am and all I am becoming. I send my signal into the world, letting all who are meant for me to be drawn and magnetized to my love and my light. I will step forward and create from where I am RIGHT NOW, not in some future version of me, not planning for when, but being right now. Stepping forward. Tiny steps. One. Little. Step. I will keep stepping one foot in front of the other and create from where I am."

This felt resonant, but something was still missing and I kept asking, "Show me what it is I need to do to fully release the tension and the pain so that I can step forward, take action, and move into my being. Show me what is here for my attention and my devotion.

Show me what needs to be released. Show me what I need to receive."

Suddenly, I was transported back to that house with the dirt floors where I had been in my mind's eye when I was unconscious. A part of me was still there in the corner. Fetal position intact. Weeping, worn out and alone. Greeting her there, I was in the deepest state of gratitude.

I was crying so hard as I spoke to her, "Thank you for choosing to live. I have so much gratitude. Thank you. I know how hard it is. I am so sorry. Thank you for trusting me. I hope you feel honored in all the space I have given you. I know it's been so hard. I am so glad you chose to be here. Thank you. I see you. I acknowledge you." I was sobbing intensely as I spoke to this part of me. "I am always going to consider you. I know you have been through so much. I will never forget you and all that it has taken you to show up every day. You have been so brave every day. I am so proud of you. You have fought so hard to just be here. Thank you for fighting so hard. I see you. You don't have to fight anymore. I'm here. We don't have to fight so hard anymore. Let's just be here. Let's be in the ease of here. The peace of here. Let's just be right here. Let's share about right here. Let people in, right here. You don't have to be perfect. I don't have to be perfect. Just show up. Let's talk about it. Let's tell your story. Let's talk about how hard it's been. You are here. You stayed. I love you so much." There was so much weeping, a pure release of emotion for how hard it has been, how few really know that and how much I need to be acknowledged in it.

In this exchange, I felt profound gratitude. Through this breathwork journey, I integrated a part of me that was stuck in the space of my subconscious. She did not want to come back to this body and, respectfully, it has been very hard to be in my body. Through the breath, I was able to really acknowledge this part of me who possibly knew it was going to be hard and just didn't want to do it.

I have given so much space for grief. I have come to realize that to be where you are and to be fully alive and fully aligned, fully able to love from right where you are, you have to give space to the parts of you that are kicking and screaming to be here in it.

Some people may call that negativity, but I have given space for what feels like grief. And in this breathwork session, I was transported back to the space that I remember being in when I was unconscious at the scene of my accident. I was there with this part of me. I held her and cried her tears. After some time, she stood up, walked out of that room, and I felt her fully integrate back into my body. This is the magic of breathwork. This is the magic of Breath of Gold.

In these 6 years, I have learned the necessary power of now more than ever before. The more HERE I can be, the more ok I am. Ok within my body, ok within these circumstances, trusting the unfolding of my life. One of the greatest treasures of breathwork for me has been the ease in which it allows me to be here, in the now. It brings me into my body and in connection with my soul. The gift of being in my body is not to be overlooked, as the number of things "wrong" or painful in this vessel are many, and the ongoing work to stay present is tremendous. Breathwork makes it feel easy. It is as if for a few moments, the vessel of my body melds into the strength and guidance of my spirit and I can just BE. If there is pain, I allow it to lead me to inquiry, and without fail, my body gives me the message that I need to understand and release.

Another session that feels particularly memorable in my healing journey was a recorded session I was doing on my own time from the Breath of Gold Breathwork Membership library. Before the circular-connected breathwork journey began, Adrienne invited us to imagine ourselves in a cocoon. This resonated with me and the imagery came easily. After a few minutes here, she invited us to stand and do whatever movement we felt led to do to break free from the cocoon and spread the wings of the beautiful butterfly that we are. I couldn't move. I lay immobilized as she continued to guide with energy building in the vibration of breaking free. I cried gently, but did not feel defeat. I felt recognition. Deep knowing. Genuine acceptance.

I heard a voice in my mind say, *"You are still in the cocoon. It is not yet time to break free and spread those wings."*

I used my voice to declare in response, *"Here is where I am, and here is where I am supposed to be. Be here, Kara."*

This particular journey of the breath was a beautiful and gentle presence in my body, knowing that the more I can occupy the actual place that I am in, the more likely I will one day be able to move and create from here. You must be fully present to the place you are in to truly carve your path forward from that place. Breath assists me in this ongoing endeavor to present myself with the acceptance of my now.

At that time in my journey, there was an ongoing theme of dead branches showing up in my environment. Bushes that had been hit hard by a week-long freeze at temps too low for them to survive. Some of them lived, but were left with the skeleton of what they were and tiny new growths at their base. These images in nature had been guiding me, as it felt like a pure reflection of what was happening in my life. My old self was like the skeleton of branches... and the tiny growth coming up was protected by its old form until it was time to trim back the dead branches in order for the new ones to grow.

In a breathwork session during this time, I was holding the intention of connecting to myself right here, right now. Amid all the trauma and everything that had happened to me, I wanted to show up in gratitude for exactly where I am on the journey.

The breath always guides me to what I need. Mid-session, Adrienne mentioned a visual of a tree and my mind went immediately to a tree in my backyard which was partly destroyed by a storm a few summers ago. I had the dead part removed and was shocked to see how fast the new shoots of growth appeared, creating an entirely new form!

I start speaking, *"I am releasing what is old. What is old was once vibrant, but now it is dead. Trimming allows for new growth. Give me the images of my new growth. I let go of anything that was the old me that is no longer growing. I am trimming the branches as I speak. I am ready. No more energy is going to what is dead. Trim the dead branches, watch the new life grow. I am open to the new."*

I think addressing parts of our being and giving space for them is so important, so I added gratitude to the old me for creating such abundance and making it so hard for me to let go of all that I knew because it was all so beautiful.

I assured her, *"You come with me in this new growth. Everything that I built was an expression of me and all of ME comes with me wherever I go. This is not a compromised version of me. It is a NEW version of me. I bring all of me here in the now so that I can build from here with all of me. Flowing from here. I haven't lost anything. I am here in wholeness, and from here I can create. I release that which I created, that is no longer living. I release the dead branches, bringing my fullness into now."*

I could feel a deep willingness to stay right here for as long as needed. I released fear of timing. I released all that was in order to open to all that is.

And then I heard, *"It is ok to cut back and be who you are. This is the liberation. This is the adjusting of your environment, and your form. Everything is different, from the way you are being in the world to what you are expecting of yourself. You cannot expect the same things from yourself, because you are changed. You have to work with what you are in this human form. If you come into reality with where you are, you can create from here."*

I felt complete acceptance of now, unlike anything I have ever experienced before. I was breathing in the now. "I trim all the expectations, other people's view of who I am, other projections of who I should be. I am allowing for the strength and stamina of my body from right here. I remain open to new ways of doing things, new ways of being, thinking and creating. My creative brain is different. I remain open to the newness of me."

At the end of the session, I heard *"Kara, I accept you right here, right now. I accept you where you are. I don't need you to grow into the old person you were. I need you to grow into the person you are becoming. Nothing is holding you back. You are completely free."*

Breathwork brings me into a beautiful dance with the Divine. For me, the breath has been a force of life that connects me to all that is and fosters clear guidance and direction. Sometimes, the guidance is very specific and sometimes it is more of a knowing or feeling I can hold in my body. I use my voice to activate things that are present in that connection. Oftentimes, the things that are revealing themselves to me in my life come alive in a breathwork session. I speak aloud anything that comes through me. I ask for specific guidance and receive messages of truth and depths of healing in response. Whether I am calling out to the people who will fill my coaching programs or speaking over my own being, I ask and listen. This is the dance.

Breathwork allows for an activation of my voice. It sets in motion an easy flow of personalized and relevant affirmations for my life, and I speak and feel into being the things that I am calling in. I release resistance to what is, release ancestral vows or anything else that reveals itself as holding me back. I discover places of deeply held emotion in my body and give space to release them, and if needed, to further understand them. I ask for and receive everything from parenting guidance to business clarity or just to enjoy a gentle, profound connection to my physical vessel. Using my breath, I declare the fullness of where I am in this moment while calling in and visualizing a future where I am fulfilled and surrounded by love and support. I make beautiful declarations of alignment, clarity, and safety for my body. And so, it is.

Simona Luna

Flow with the River

Yesterday, I completely lost my voice.

This has only happened a few times in my life—and exactly now, as I'm about to start writing for this book... (what an irony!) If there are no coincidences, what's the message?

I am grateful to be blessed with a healthy body, but my throat has always been my weakest point. Whenever I'd get sick, it would be with a sore throat, tonsillitis, or an ongoing cough...

I had never really thought about it until I started learning about our energy body. Then it struck me that this was clearly connected to a block in my throat chakra.

(Little did I know that one day I would become a teacher, coach, and speaker – and I'm now using my voice all the time to express myself and inspire others)

Looking back on my life, I can see how it makes sense...

As a child, I felt like I literally lost my voice.

I grew up in Vienna in the 80s in a middle-class family. Both of my parents were doing their best, but they were struggling with their mental health and their own unresolved trauma. Their relationship became more and more manipulative and toxic over the years. Apart from some holidays or special events, I hardly have memories of us doing things together as a family.

My father was away for work a lot and I spent most of my time with my mother raising me. She was strict and controlling. I didn't feel as if my wishes and desires were really taken into account. I was told to be quiet, shut up, and obey.

I remember how my dad once ridiculed me for apparently singing so terribly in the school choir. I was so embarrassed and hurt that I stopped singing altogether.

Growing up, I often felt scared and intimidated by my mum's sudden outbursts of rage. Within an instant, she could turn from a loving, lively woman into an unrecognizable, out-of-control lunatic. She would scream at my dad when they were fighting, and throw dishes around the house... while he was standing there laughing at her.

I was a shy, sensitive girl and turned more and more inward.

I had to learn to look after myself and manage my own emotions when my primary caregivers were not able to provide the nurturing care and unconditional love I was craving.

My survival strategy became to comply and be the "good girl". I didn't feel safe at home, so I started trying to control my environment and managing the people around me. I found myself constantly anticipating my mum's needs and caring for her emotionally. It gave me a sense of control in an unpredictable world—but left my own self-worth shattered.

Only now—after decades of healing, personal development, and deep inner work—do I understand how much both of my parents were carrying.

Now, I can see how each time my throat was swelling up, burning from an inflammation, energetically it was releasing another layer of ancestral trauma from generations before me.

Lifetimes of suppression and being silenced. Fear of speaking the unspeakable.

Each time an old layer was cleared to fall away, there was a sense of opening and expansion.

Slowly I could start finding my true expression.

To finally liberate my voice and speak my truth.

While I was always curious about spirituality, my own healing journey really began with my divorce when I was twenty-nine. My Saturn Return. It was what they call the *"dark night of the soul"* and a radical turning point in my life.

I was coming out of a five-year long complicated relationship where I had completely lost and abandoned myself. As I was picking up the pieces, trying to understand why this had happened, I started therapy and embarked on my yoga journey.

Yoga literally came to my rescue at this time. I started a daily vigorous Ashtanga practice, which left me exhausted in sweat and tears... but at least I felt alive again!

It was time to begin a new chapter of choosing myself.

I moved to London.

Working as a designer and art director in the creative industries by day, I dedicated my evenings and weekends to yoga workshops, kirtan, and spiritual talks where I got to experience masters from HH Dalai Lama, Thích Nhất Hạnh, and Deepak Chopra. In order to escape the stress of my day job in the agencies, I started taking long trips to India, Thailand, and Bali.

What a contrast. I tasted a completely different way of life.

Soon, I followed the call for more freedom.

I made the decision to quit my job and started my first business as a freelance designer, which allowed me to escape the winter for two months each year to fully immerse myself in my spiritual journey.

In a co-working space in Bali, I met my first coach who helped me with my new company Moon Tribe, an ethical clothing brand. I had launched this business to escape the corporate world once and for all... but as it was growing, I ended up completely overwhelmed and on the edge of burnout.

That was when I experienced the power of coaching for the first time.

Life kept guiding me toward my purpose, and one thing led to the next.

I started realizing my natural gifts for deep listening, energetic alchemy, and seeing the true potential in others. And I was passionate about empowering women after my own journey of deep healing and reclaiming my self-worth.

Soon after, I made the decision to completely change my career and follow my passion full-time. I was in my late thirties.

After nine years, I left London and moved to Amsterdam.

A new chapter began and I started dedicating myself to teaching yoga and helping new entrepreneurs to create freedom for themselves as a Spiritual Business Coach.

As part of my yoga teacher training, I had been learning about the moon and how to follow its cycle. Soon, working with the lunar / yin / feminine energy became a natural focus in my work.

More and more, I realized the unhealthy grip of patriarchal conditioning in our lives—impacting the way we think, work, treat our body, make love, or relate to nature. I saw so much distortion around the feminine—with both women and men suffering from it.

For me, healing came in different stages of balancing the divine feminine and divine masculine energies—within myself, in my business, and in my relationship with my partner.

(And it's an ongoing process...)

While my mind still has a tendency to run back into old patterns, while my voice still struggles sometimes to fully express itself, my body already knows what it means to be free.

I just need to turn up the music, dance, and surrender to the wisdom of my body.

I just need to go for a swim in the ocean.

I just need to lie in the sun and listen to the birds.

My body knows how to feel pleasure.

It's her natural state.

It's our natural state.

(Just look at a child playing or a cat taking a nap.)

Yet, there are times when I fall asleep and forget all of this.

In the last weeks, my mind has been playing these games with me again.

Luring me into doing mode.

Keeping me busy.

Adding one more thing to my to-do list.

Convincing me that only by controlling everything I'll be safe.

Instead of swimming, I caught myself pushing the river.

This has been a pattern on my entrepreneurial journey… (and I thought I had mastered it!)

But they say you'll encounter the same old limitations again and again at various stages. At first, they might appear different… but then turn out as yet another layer of the same old fear or self-sabotage you know too well.

And you get to go deeper—into the next level of mastery.

As I saw this old pattern creeping up again I've been reflecting: why am I still doing this?

Overworking, pushing, running…

I know it's old. And I know it's not what I want. I'm ready to release this once and for all… and allow myself to relax and receive on a deeper level.

To prioritize pleasure, enjoy life, and trust the flow.

So as we began the breathwork journey that Adrienne guided us through, I set my intention…

To release control.

I began breathing deeply, inhaling and exhaling through my mouth. I moved through resistance. Then I got into the flow… and the breath started breathing me.

I could feel my consciousness shifting.

A higher intelligence took over that can see the bigger picture.

And then I had an unexpected and shocking realization.

I suddenly saw how deep this pattern runs in my family... it's not even mine!

In an instant, its roots were revealed to me.

The painful, complete loss of control that both my mother and my grandmother had to endure... when they were sexually assaulted and abused as a child.... by someone they had loved and trusted. Their desperate struggle to regain a sense of control their whole life, feeling so lost.

I could feel their pain.

The emptiness... nothing to hold on to.

A sense of staring into the abyss.

Facing the darkest shadows of this human experience.

I felt tears flowing down my face.

My heart burst wide open.

I felt a huge sense of forgiveness and love for both of them.

I could see how this deep wounding of the feminine was the root of so much suffering for the women in my family... the heavy trauma we've been carrying until today.

On a soul level, a powerful scene started unfolding before my eyes.

I saw each one of us as a soul, a being of light—my mother, my sister, my aunt, my cousin. First, everyone was struggling separately and alone..... but slowly we started coming together in a circle, hugging each other tightly, healing, feeling safe.

Around us appeared the men in my family who are firmly rooted in the sacred masculine—my partner, my father, my cousin—forming a circle of protection together with angels.

After a while, I saw the other women in my family appear who were healthy and uncompromised in their feminine essence—my other grandmother with her sisters, my grand aunts. They gathered to form a circle around us... and I received their healing codes.

I could feel a huge sense of forgiveness wash over me.

My heart was wide open.

I was able to see my mum's journey in a new light and forgive her on a completely new level.

Finally, I let go of the blame I've been carrying for so long.

I surrendered to love.

As we slowly returned back into our bodies, I was feeling a sense of lightness and ease.

I saw myself lying back into the big river of life, letting its current carry me.

It's safe for me to trust life. I don't need to push or force.

Simply flow with the river...

Amy Quinn

Freeing Myself from an Addictive Lover

I started breathwork two years ago, when I found myself trapped in a trauma-bond, a dynamic I felt powerless to escape. Before entering this relationship, I considered myself to be one of the most strong, free-spirited, adventurous people alive: I surfed ten-foot waves over protruding coral heads in Indonesia; I mountain biked through lava fields competing in the Maui Xterra World Championships; I camped solo in the Appalachian wilderness. Furthermore, I had an amazing network of family and friends in a community that loved and supported me. There was no goal I felt like I couldn't reach, and no challenge I felt like I couldn't overcome. Perhaps I felt most invincible in my ability to control my emotions; I felt unbreakable—until I met a man who found the chink in my armor—my achilles heel.

I met my pathological partner in the winter of 2019, shortly after separating from my husband of twenty years. I had married at the age of twenty-one— a rushed decision that I started to question the night of my wedding. We weren't emotionally compatible partners, but we shared many common interests—including our love of outdoor adventures. I fell in love with the life we lived on a beautiful barrier island off the coast of North Carolina, where we raised our three children. Looking back, the emotional distance between us felt safe; vulnerability was not my strong suit. Furthermore, we were so detached by the time we divorced that the process was peaceful. I had grieved the death of the marriage long before the divorce papers were signed. However, the consequence of staying in a relationship long past its expiration date is a numb heart. After my separation, I reminisced on my first love, a young man I had dated for seven years before dating my ex- husband. Although we were young, we shared a deep bond, and I simply wanted another chance to find true love again.
Inspired by Khalil Ghibran's poem, "On Joy and Sorrow", I penned the following words: "I want to come alive again. I want to fall in love so deeply that it hurts. I want to feel everything from deep grief to ecstatic joy."

Be careful what you pray for.

I figured it would be years before I found love again. However, my prayers were answered less than a month after entering that journal entry. My daughter was attending a new school, and I began running into him at school events.

We developed an instant friendship. He was also leaving a long-term relationship—one he claimed had died years ago—like mine. But his relationship status didn't matter to me because I wasn't initially attracted to him. In fact, I was certain I would be the one to break his heart. Yet something about the attention he gave me was intoxicating. He was constantly texting me sweet messages, leaving gifts in my car, and showering me with affection. He lived in a charming, historic downtown neighborhood on the water, where he'd wine and dine me most evenings. What finally hooked me was the way he nurtured me. I had never experienced that type of love and care, especially from a male figure. He had a deep voice, a broad chest, and a seemingly huge heart. I'd collapse into his arms and never want to leave. I felt like a bear who had never tasted honey, and all of a sudden, I was drowning in a well of it.

Within a month, we became inseparable. Outside of work, we spent every minute together. In the blink of an eye, I unknowingly abandoned myself. I quit my hobbies, withdrew from my friendships, and did the bare minimum to maintain integrity at work—a new job I was fortunate to land. Furthermore, we couldn't keep our hands off of each other. The intimacy was unlike anything I had ever experienced. I felt loved, seen, protected. It was beyond anything I could have ever dreamed.

We all know the old saying: *"If it seems too good to be true..."*

I noticed a shift in him about three months into our relationship—literally overnight. He had an intense, emotional argument with his son late one Friday evening in early May, but seemed fine by the time we went to bed. We woke up the next morning and went to look at a house together. Then we parted ways for a few hours while I attended my son's lacrosse game. When I saw him again later that afternoon, he seemed like a different person. The strong, loving, protective partner with whom I had fallen in love suddenly felt like a scared child. His enormous heart had shrunk; I couldn't find it. Where he had originally been vibrant and charismatic, he was now withdrawn and depressed. He started telling me he was questioning the relationship, wondering if we had moved too fast, suggesting we should be friends.

My head started spinning. We had looked at a house together hours earlier. He had called me a dozen times the day before to tell me how much he loved me. We slept tangled up in each other the night before. Now he was hinting at breaking up with me?

In a fog, I packed the things I had at his house and went back to the space I was renting—confused and devastated.

I didn't know what the hell was going on. I just knew something was deeply wrong. For a month after that, we continued to see each other regularly, but the dynamic of the relationship was different. He was different. I questioned him about his ex-girlfriend, but he swore that it was over and that he had not talked to her since they had broken up. He continued to assure me that he was in love with me and that he wanted to spend his life with me; he claimed he was simply struggling with issues related to his son, who would be graduating high school soon. I gave him space, confident the man I'd fallen in love would return.

Within a month, he started to seem like his normal self again, and I began to exhale a sigh of relief. He came to stay with me at my beach house on a Wednesday evening in early June, and I distinctly remember him talking about getting married. When he left the next morning, we planned to meet for dinner after he got off work. Sitting at the restaurant, I texted him when he was ten minutes late. He responded: *"Amy, I'm sorry. My ex and I went to counseling today, and we are going to try to reconcile. Please do not ever contact me again."*

A jolt of electricity surged through my body. I didn't know that amount of shock was possible. What was happening? Was this a nightmare? Had I fallen in love with a sociopath? I didn't know what to do with myself. I hopped in my car and drove five hours from my coastal town to the mountains to stay with a dear friend. Sleep was elusive anyhow.

Within two days, he was texting again, deeply apologetic. He begged for another chance. He told me he felt sorry for his ex and was guilted into going to counseling with her. He claimed she had taken his phone when I texted him, and she had typed those messages. In his plea for forgiveness, he offered to go to counseling with me. He showed me a text he sent her telling her he was in love with me and did not want to be back together with her.

I agreed to see him a couple of days later when I returned from the mountains, and suddenly, he was back to his charismatic, vibrant self. I left for a trip to Ireland the following week, and he went to see my therapist before I even got back. When I returned from my trip, he whisked me away on a romantic trip to a secluded cabin outside of Asheville. We spent a glorious day at the Grove Park Inn and Spa. We swam in waterfalls. We lounged on a screened-in sleeping porch and watched fireflies every evening. The dynamic felt more magical than ever. I pretty much moved into his house when we returned, and we spent a blissful summer together, taking several other trips. We did couples counseling as he promised. My therapist, whom I deeply trusted, assured me how deeply he loved me; he said he could see it and feel it. He compared the incident with his ex-girlfriend to a *"speed bump"*—the aftermath and confusion of leaving a long-term relationship, mixed with major changes he was experiencing as a parent. I tried to allow his words to comfort me, but when I was completely honest with myself, there was a constant undercurrent of unrest. The incident from earlier in the summer continued to haunt me, and I was worried he would spiral down again.

Sure enough, by the end of the summer, he began to shift. One Friday night in early August, we skipped town for the night on yet another romantic date to the famous Chef and The Farmer. We talked the entire evening. We created a game where we'd try to guess the names of people in the restaurant. We ordered four desserts and laughed until our stomachs hurt. But things quickly went south when—at some point later that weekend—I brought up the *"speed bump"* we had encountered earlier in the summer. The conversation triggered him, and by the end of the week, a dark cloud, reminiscent of the one I'd witnessed earlier that spring, was starting to settle over him.

We dropped his son off at college days later, a moment he had been dreading. The following Monday, he called me on his way home from work and told me he was thinking about his ex-girlfriend again. She had also dropped her youngest son off at college, and he said he was worried about her being alone. Within a week, not only did he disappear, but he blocked me. And this time, he didn't call two days later. In fact, I didn't hear from him for two months.

I had felt bonded to him in a primal way, and the rejection I experienced manifested as physical pain. I felt like he had pushed me off a steep cliff, then turned his back and walked away. Every bone in my body felt broken. I was a shell of the person I had been before I met him. I didn't know how to move forward with my life. While friends and family showered me with love and support, none of it brought me comfort. Their love rolled off of me like water off a duck. I was addicted to the nectar only he could provide. Enter the trauma-bond– an addiction formed from intermittent reinforcement–more powerful than a heroin addiction.

At this point, I knew that I had fallen in love with a deeply broken man, and I was bound and determined to figure out what I had gotten myself into. I went on a rampage studying trauma, mood disorders, and personality disorders. I came across a site on Borderline Personality Disorder, and I began to make sense of my situation. While everything I was reading was telling me to run like hell, I just wanted him back, and I knew he would come back. I was determined to wait in that dark place until he returned.

I ran into him downtown a couple of months later, but he didn't even look like himself. He asked if I would be willing to sit down and talk. He confessed that after the two of us had broken up, he had committed himself into an inpatient facility because he felt like he was having a nervous breakdown. His diagnosis matched my suspicion. He shared that he was hiding the severity of his mental instability while we were dating. I felt deep compassion for him— and I felt vindicated.

We began to see each other regularly again. One night I asked him if anything traumatic had ever happened to him. His body began to tremble and he wept as he told me about an assault he had suffered as a young adult. At one point I asked, *"You did process this with the therapists in the hospital, right?"*

He looked at me confused, then shook his head no. "I've never told anyone except my parents."

I was perplexed. He had been diagnosed and medicated, yet no one had begun to unearth the root of his trauma?

I pleaded with him to go to therapy to specifically process his assault. He agreed without hesitation. We found a therapist who practiced EMDR, and he was excited about finally dealing with his past. I thought, *"Maybe he doesn't have a personality disorder. Maybe his behavior is the result of PTSD."* I felt genuine hope. We spent an enchanting Christmas together. He spoiled my kids and me like Santa Claus would, gifting me my beloved Australian labradoodle, Joy, and a suitcase full of Free People clothes. Furthermore, I had purchased an adorable cottage earlier that fall, and he moved his things into my house in January. The third round was even more intense than the second.

But like clockwork, after a couple of months, the dark cloud returned. He began to mention his ex, and the downward spiral was repeating a third time.

Unlike the other times where I was simply confused and hurt, I began to grow angry. I was starting to witness a side of him I hadn't observed before. While he was withdrawn and depressed the first couple of rounds, he became cold, even mean at times. I was witnessing a deceitful, manipulative side to him.

More of his true colors were beginning to be revealed.

For the first time, I told myself I wouldn't take him back. Little did I know how deeply I was addicted to him—to the cycle. In addition, my environment created a vacuum. Covid was sweeping the world, and I was working from home. Living in a new town on quarantine, I was lonely–and bored out of my mind. He'd show up at my door with a flower bouquet, twinkling eyes, and a huge grin. In those moments, I'd only see the man with whom I'd originally fallen in love, and I'd completely block out the dark side that lingered under the surface. I'd be tangled up with him within an hour. The cognitive dissonance was staggering.

I knew the cycle was insane. I knew I shouldn't take him back—that it wouldn't end well—but he became a force I couldn't overcome. I felt like a little surfer girl bobbing in the ocean, and he was a powerful tsunami. Each time the tidal wave would roll in, I'd willingly surrender and submit to the exhilaration of the wave, which gave me an adrenaline high unlike anything I'd ever experienced. But like all waves, it would inevitably begin to break. As it would start to crumble, I'd be dragged down in the dark undertow, tossing and turning in a dark swirl of chaos, fear gripping every cell of my body. At the peak of my terror and vulnerability, the whitewater would slam me down violently on the shore, breaking every bone in my body, leaving me parched and dehydrated in the scorching sun. I'd lie there in a trance, praying for the tide to rise again, pull me back out to sea, and comfort me with its gentle rocking waves. But it never came, at least when I needed it most. In fact, it wouldn't come back until I'd gather up the strength to dust myself off and start walking away. Just when I thought I'd reached safety at the dune line, the tsunami would cover me over and sweep me back out to sea.

A pathological partner doesn't want you back until they think they're losing you. Those who have been in a relationship like this know this destructive scenario all too well.

I'm embarrassed to share how many times this cycle repeated. I began to lose faith in myself. However, I finally realized there was something deeply broken in me that was allowing the insanity to perpetuate. I began to focus less on him and more on myself.

I realized that I needed to face the deep wounds and abandonment I had endured as a child. As an enneagram seven, I had spent my entire life avoiding pain. In fact, I didn't cry at all from the ages of four to eighteen, and very little in my adulthood. I knew deep down that if I was ever going to end this abusive cycle, I had to face my core wounds and feel their pain in order to heal.

The journey back to myself culminated when I did a three-day therapeutic retreat with a specialist to deal with my childhood trauma. I received a wealth of insight on the common threads and patterns in my life, especially as it related to the males in my sphere. I could see that the chaos I was playing out with my partner mirrored the primary relationships I had as a child.

After that weekend, I began to read every book I could find about inner child healing. I started to meditate. I wrote in my journal daily. I had been a yoga teacher for twenty years, but I started practicing more regularly. I spent hours in nature. With the combination of these healing tools, I did notice subtle shifts. I was regaining my power and holding stronger boundaries, but not strong enough to hold him back completely.

I realized I needed to take more extreme measures. I had always wanted to live in the mountains, so I sold my house and moved seven hours across the state for a fresh start.

However, not even a drastic move could stop the cycle. The hurricane that had caused the tidal waves simply moved inland.

I'd justify each reconciliation. He continued regular therapy and even attended a two-week intensive in Colorado. I'd repeat the following narrative, *"He's doing the work. I know he really loves me. His ex-girlfriend is a safe, older, motherly figure to whom he runs when he's feeling depressed or insecure (his narrative). We have a rare connection. I'll never love like this again."* In the good moments, I was still able to block out the negative times, which I now understand was a trauma response. But with each breakup, my hope would be shattered. Losing even more faith in myself, I started to dip into a despair. I prayed desperately for a key to freedom.

My answer arrived within weeks when I discovered breathwork—specifically conscious connected breathing. I started attending an online breathwork circle every Friday evening. The first thing I noticed was that I was able to become present in the moment. Like anyone dealing with heartbreak, I had been constantly ruminating on the past or projecting into the future—living in a state of fear. During breathwork, even if it was just for a few minutes, I discovered what it was like for my nervous system to be at rest. Observing this peaceful contrast, I realized I had lived my entire life with a buzz of anxiety coursing through my body, which I dealt with by staying busy, running from the uncomfortable emotions that always lingered there under the surface. Through breathing, I learned to be present and still with my discomfort instead of running away from it or numbing it.

I also began to experience what it was like to delve deep inside my body and get in touch with the subtle sensations there. I noticed the places that were open, and those that were constricted. I learned that my body is always communicating with me, and that the constricted areas where tension resided were warning signals telling me where I wasn't living in alignment with my highest self. I began to ask my body questions. I learned that she never lies, so I began to trust her.

My intuition became sharper, and I struggled to lie to myself. One time I was driving toward his house, and I began to feel dizzy. It's like an invisible wall was erected in the middle of the highway. I pulled over on the side of the road in a panic. I started deep breathing, but I couldn't regulate myself. No amount of breathing will calm the body when one is headed toward danger. My body was warning, *"No, don't go there!"*

I experienced states of euphoria during breathwork, which was a much healthier alternative than other numbing tactics I had tried. Those moments of bliss were a balm for my aching heart.

Furthermore, every time I breathed, it felt like I was pouring fresh water into a murky stream, and little by little, my system began to clear of the trauma I was carrying. As I discharged the fear and shame, I was experiencing a higher vibration of peace and joy, which was causing the low vibration relationship to become less and less palatable.

The cycles were becoming shorter and less frequent. I eventually began to date someone else—a healthy partner. When that relationship ended several months later due to impending physical distance, I went back to my pathological partner one final time. But I felt like I was suffocating. There was no flow in my life. I felt heavy and lethargic all the time. When I finally walked away eight months ago, I knew it was for good. The universe had been patient with me until that point while I had learned the lessons I needed to learn, but I had a feeling that going back again would have detrimental consequences for my bright future.

The final key to my freedom involved forgiveness. I was intensely angry with him, but I was more angry with myself for subjecting myself to the chaotic cycle for five years. I didn't want to live with resentment in my heart, and I didn't want to feel like I was always bracing for his inevitable return. My intention was to be set free, once and for all.

I attended Adrienne's life-changing breathwork retreat in Sedona. During the first session, I had a vision of him as a child—pure and innocent—and I was able to have compassion for him. Then I was taken back to a positive memory of him, and probably the only time when his highest self was online. He had just returned from a therapeutic men's retreat in Colorado, and he seemed free and full of light. Meeting him in that higher place, I could feel a sincere apology. Within minutes, the song "I'm Sorry" began to play. Adrienne intuitively came over and began to hold me while I wept. Tears flowed like a river as the anger that was protecting my heartache began to dissipate. Grief released from my body and deep forgiveness washed over me. After the session, my heart was vulnerable from shedding the protective layers of anger. However, I didn't feel drawn to the relationship anymore. The cognitive dissonance that I had previously experienced was no longer present. While I had only seen black or white before, I could see both sides of him clearly. I could hold him in compassion and forgiveness while realizing that he is far from being able to hold me safely in a relationship, as he primarily lives in a state of shame and fear.

During the last session of the retreat, I experienced a profound energetic shift. Bright light began to infiltrate every cell of my being. It felt like lingering wounds were washed over with pure, white snow. I was able to fully forgive myself and visualize a fresh start for my life.

I now realize that the brutal journey on which I embarked five years ago had been divinely guided from the start. An answer to my original prayer, I encountered the one person who could aim his arrow precisely at that one tiny crack in my armor, and crumbled the concrete walls I'd spent a lifetime erecting. The gift I found there among the rubble was my precious heart that had been wounded forty years earlier. Throughout this healing journey, I have learned to hold it with compassion and tenderness, and it has healed and opened with a much greater capacity for love and joy.

Breaking this trauma-bond has been exponentially harder than any other challenge I've ever faced. The waves of grief have felt like relentless contractions. I kept thinking, *"Something beautiful has to be birthed from all of this pain."* That notion was a self-fulfilling prophecy. I'm not the same person I was five years ago. I've become a much stronger, wiser, freer version of myself. I am eternally grateful for my discovery of breathwork, which helped me labor through the darkest days of my life, and delivered me straight into the light.

Veronica Galipo

Soul Unshackling through Breath of Gold

"The wisest one-word sentence? Breathe." - Terri Guillemets

My skin is flooded with sensations; my body's energy shifts.

There is a quivering; something in me is loosening. It feels like a dance of emergence; old shackles are rattling apart and coming undone. The waves and pulses of breath are trying to throw my soul free—free from what?

I am hesitant to know, yet I feel pulled to continue.

I feel an undercurrent of intense craziness. The involuntary shudders and quivers are becoming more potent. Many Parts of me are shredding other parts of me. I am becoming soul-exposed. The energy-filled tears begin gently, streaming down the side of my face, beginning to pattern the sheets more and more sacredly.

My body is thrown with every vibrational shift.

This ecstatic horizontal dance of beat and body escalates in tempo, and the tears of soul-filled sadness fall harder; my overwhelming expression builds, and my cries peak to a higher awareness of something inside me. I am being initiated into a new truth. And all of my soul knows it is time.

I am all in.

The jolts of the external world had broken me so many times that they had taken their toll. The year before last, as the world was somewhat calamitous, I found myself with the possibility of nowhere to live. I was packing up our rented home, filling the container with both my things and the children's belongings. I was struggling to find another home, as the market had become extremely competitive. My body began to show a recurrence of signs of my past, intense symptoms of pain, enduring prolonged illnesses, and persistent ailments. The final straw was the coughing that bruised my diaphragm to possible rib damage; this constriction affected not only my freedom to move and talk but, sadly, my breath, suffocating the ease of life itself.

I now know that this was an accumulation of years of staying small and pleasing everyone, preventing me from placing any possible burdens on others. I was aware of this character default long before this current crisis. Ten years ago, I was in a 15-year relationship; the years started light and joyous. Fairly quickly, they were filled with my partner battling a stressful, busy company alongside an egotistic business partner, our two young children, and my work. I was not coping; my body and mind were failing. We had drifted, and I felt very alone. I finally found the courage to share my heavy fears of my feelings of failure as a mother, how I felt our relationship was being affected, and how I was struggling to function. Unfortunately, my partner was dismissive after my soulful and vulnerable outpour of concerns and explanation of my worries. He didn't seem to think there was a problem and thought all would be fine.

At first, I accepted that this was totally my issue; it was my responsibility to fix everything. I turned to blaming myself and seeking guidance from therapists; the self-blame and self-attacking continued, and what sadly unfolded was a lot of internal anger and loss. Three years after this day of voicing my fears and truths, I started to believe that the only person who had my back was me, yet I had no idea what that meant.

This uncertainty affected my interactions with people, which felt more complex; I battled constant indecisiveness, and coping with all life's basic responsibilities felt monstrous and exhausting. I was yearning for someone to hold me up and guide me to some soul peace, both awake and asleep. I'd had enough of feeling alone to fight this battle. I was so worn out. Unfortunately, the distance grew, and the awareness that what I felt was critical wasn't being heard was when all of me knew it was time to have my back and leave.

Through many tosses, turns, and new awarenesses of myself, after a few years of beginning to heal, here I was, feeling stranded. My last resort was living with my dad, which I hadn't done for 30+ years. He was a true Italian man who worked hard and had quite a set and serious demeanor most of the time, causing a unique and trying experience.

However, I knew he loved me in his own way and of course having a roof over my head was a blessing. Not only was I in new, uncertain circumstances, but I was also living in a different area, which altered how often I would see my divine young teenage boys, which, as you can imagine, added to my heaviness.

With all this, I questioned: *"Why me? When will things let up?"*

During this time, I was desperately seeking respite and a way out. My core was screaming: enough was ENOUGH. I reached for options and began looking for courses and workshops to break through where I had found myself. In the past, I was fortunate to have done some energy and bodywork and learned its powerful effects, including different breathing methods.

Breathwork intrigued me; my introduction was mainly through online examples of coaches who shared short and intense styles; they felt too foreign or did not align, and I hoped there were other styles; then I tasted the gentle yet powerful Breath of Gold style. I was blessed to be introduced to Adrienne at the right time. My first encounter was through an online challenge with information, interviews, and daily breathwork journeys.

It wasn't just what Adrienne shared, but how she shared it that made her so compelling. Her stories were raw and honest, her guidance delivered gentleness and kindness. Adrienne guided each session with a unique play of layered music and divine lead singing; her flow of divinely molded messages and guidance was so gentle, which resonated with me at this most vulnerable time. I knew I could only take this soul-freeing voyage toward the true me, 'Veronica,' in a caring, passive way, and this dance of breath, music, rhythm, and guidance was the beginning of my being's freedom and release. I was awestruck by the realization that something as fundamental as my breath could hold the key to such a profound shift.

First, I committed to her 12-week journey of golden guidance through breathwork and journaling. In the middle of these sessions, I realised how each prompt aligned with my need to be centred and clear.

During the first few guided breathworks, I felt cautious. I could feel the uncertainty of what could happen. Then, finally, the time came for this sacred ride- my much-awaited escape. It came with a desperate, deliberate need to take over.

'Passive' obviously wasn't the only way; I started all rugged up and still, laying on my bed, then I began to feel tingles as I had in the past and then began to tremble. I felt my legs dancing on their own as they had somewhere to go or desire to be set free; they twitched and flicked. With each deep breath, my entire existence at this point is being willed to move; my hands stiffen and cramp with each gasp of breath, my back arches, and my whole body is willed to shift and lift with another exhale; all this felt like it was happening to me and with me, why or how I am not sure only that I surrender to every pull.

I lay sprawled on my bed, attacks of intense waves rattling, rocking, and shaking my old energy, ripping me apart, taking over me while rippling through the walls. This home, finally just mine for a week, felt like it was also holding its own breath.

I had never felt this intensity through breathwork; it was a more profound soul-revealing experience. It's unbelievable how much I had endured. Two home births, one which lasted 36 hours of exhausting waves. Unexpected panic attacks that shook me to the ground. The breakdown of my 22-year relationship, the separation that wounded more than just us. Each challenge felt like a mountain to climb, and I was exhausted. The weight of it all felt insurmountable.I was struggling to fathom what was stuck, what I feared that was keeping me ensnared from the freedom of my true spirit.

Then, a deep wave of sadness and grief surfaced, and I became aware of how I had diminished myself most of my life, convincing myself I wasn't strong enough to cope or thrive. Yet, against these beliefs, I had an innate knowing to trust and push through no matter the obstacles. Surprisingly, this gave me an internal stance of proof that I could be capable of far more than I had ever imagined. I felt an unveiling of myself and movement to another level.

This center-core circular breathing, which had such a powerful grip this time, amplified every sensation; I felt intense dread about how I had had enough. Then, with this Angel, Adrienne's, guidance through this solo breathwork session, I felt like I was in a new, refined dance, giving myself undeniable permission: NO MORE. It was a do-or-die, go-all-in type of conviction.

I had no choice but to uncage what I had held onto for so long.

My body was shaking stronger; my need, my unwavering determination to push, to hold the breathing pattern, got deeper. I literally could feel my mind getting broken apart from some stuck, trapped, locked hold on unconscious chains of belief...it was happening.

I was here and elsewhere through this trance of wild awakening; It was both so desirable and an overwhelming emotion of fear. I had a deep-seated hurt, and yet I seemed to embrace it, I pulled away from the ache while drawn towards the understanding.

It was tearing me away, yet it was the healing path I needed.

I felt its mountainous peak being reached. My body was being thrown, my skin shivering with each body rhythm, and each breath had its own frenzied beat. This dance was so unknown to all of me; the breathing was leading my body, dipping and dropping the depths of me every which way, all the while my soul vigorously sought it so eagerly, waiting for the finale.

I'm crying; my tears an avalanche of rawness, my whole being is mourning..and then a hollow, intense, deep, gritted roar, an outpour of:

"I AM Enough...I AM Enough! Ahhhhh, NO MORE proving, no more NEEDING to do!"

Oh, it was so sad, the deep whaling of my tears, the shedding of emotion, the releasing of truth, yet so wildly awakening. My awakening, finally an ignite of my rights to just be me. Free of proving, free of trying, free of approval: FREE, FREE, FREE of what I unconsciously held. Free of a soul-historic story of having to prove my worth all my life.

From 3 years old, I carried the good girl to please and appease; I held back, chose quiet, never to contribute to what was happening around me, and felt responsible for keeping the peace. The little 'me' felt unworthy of having a voice; I needed to allow others to have their say and space. I continued to make room for others and believed others were worthy of everything. These behaviours continued for 20 years, caring for my mum and sister unconsciously, then 22 years of proving my worth in my relationship, fearing I would disappoint. All these beliefs embedded and continuously pressured me to prove my worthiness.

This was the day I began to yell myself free, freeing with decisive, deliberate anger. I finally released myself from the shackles I thought were necessary to keep me safe and prove my worth. No more, never again. DONE. No more proving I am.

I AM BLOODY ENOUGH!

I spent over an hour in this state, in convulsions of realization that I was all I needed to be. I am everything I should be as I am; All of me is all-encompassed beauty, therefore worthy of all, free of any have-to's.

Oh my god, I swear if someone had seen, heard, or felt this vulcanic elevation, they would have perceived a woman struggling and suffering, but for me, it was my true wilding essence being freed from my created cage. A cage developed from a toddler's point of view, which she had interpreted as helping others despite all of her, was the right way, and she unknowingly crazily buried herself.

This unconscious obligation took over her ways; she gave to the point of exhaustion; she continued to prove herself in hopes of acceptance and diminished herself, believing she shouldn't shine. Sadly, it prevented her from understanding boundaries and soul limits, not being able to receive and accept all her uniqueness.... but gratefully from her awakenings through her coaching profession and seeking more and more ways for soul freedom and self-sufficient foundation....she was able to embrace all of her.

Finally, the wings I had become aware of and started healing since I left my long-term relationship six years prior were finally being shaken free of any entangled, prohibited belief; now, I was giving myself permission to fly and free my soul to dance my way for the benefit of me first more than ever before. I was sadly my own trapper and now powerfully my own releaser.

This intentional breathing, this conscious opening of my lungs, was one of the most profound moments of my intense seven-year transformation. For over an hour, I resonated with an almighty therapeutic core shift of forgotten or possibly unknown self-worth. A renewed awakening energy flowed through me in peaks and wavelengths, expressing the monumental healing within. My whole being was consumed with releasing self-imposed beliefs. All was unleashed vocally and emotionally through divine empowering words.

Below, I share a small but monumental part of my heart, igniting messages that surged intensely from me that day:

I am all that I need to be. I am everything I am meant to be. That is love. I am love.

Veronica, you were given this path, gifted each step and each hiccup to get here, all to realise your true worth! Accept this universal awakening and choose this RETREAT.

Know and choose to do less, and begin to release the need for full responsibility; it's allowed, it's okay.

I am enough. I never have to push to prove. I strive to be as I am... I am as I am and it is enough.

Veronica, the YOU you are is pure love. You are worthy of being loved and devoted to. You are worthy of being given true, loyal, and prioritised love.

To receive from my giving is the way of my being. This is pure balance; the yin yang. Giving isn't complete without receiving. It is the law of love. I live and I am love.

Love flows naturally from you & to you, Veronica.

Begin today to live with an allowance to LOVE and an allowance to receive.

I am in Harmony.
When I balance my giving and being given to.
I love me for the existence of me!

As I screamed each of these phrases, I felt a raw, wilding warrior unleash her full force through my transformation. These spells have since bewitched my soul to have an inner embedded knowing—a spiritual unveiling of love and beauty for myself and to express to each soul for themselves.

This "shackled free" breathwork session opened the door to many more over the next six months." I was feeling pulled to release and be open to more experiences. The beautiful thing that began unfolding was an aligned decision on my business mission and message. The beauty is that I felt I knew the power of love from a young age, yet unfortunately, I belittled it. However, in past breakthroughs and transformational work, I awakened the essence of all my self-awareness, self-acceptance, and self-assurance.

I am now humbly embracing and devoting myself, allowing myself to listen and step into this expert space of a self-love guide and facilitator, ultimately a life-enhancing coach. My soul mission feels charged to change the world one soul-love at a time, guiding individuals to discover and embrace their own self-love, thereby creating a rippling dance of love and acceptance to flow throughout our world.

With each journal entry, each self-guided meditation, and each liberating breathwork session, I felt my soul conviction deepening. A sense of clarity emerged, a newfound strength I hadn't known I had. I started making more self-trusting choices, setting healthier boundaries, and speaking my truth with confidence. My most recent soul-dancing, soul-flying breathwork gained even stronger momentum around this vision. My inspiration behind this session was to be open and release resistance that prevented me from sharing this message. I intended to be even more aware of my creativity and step into courage.

As I began the breathing pattern, I started to sense vulnerability and self-trust; I allowed myself to feel all sensations that arose. A flow of gentle beginnings started to fill my heart, first a rawness of how I once felt so alone and estranged from myself and others. I was exquisitely bathed with gratitude and relief for my wonder and ability to love so much. This whirlwind of thoughts and feelings gave rise to a varied understanding of how I am loved and have to trust in the love I have always held in my heart but felt was foolish to share. A newfound clarity that sharing love through word, expression, guidance, and care is the key, regardless of people not being ready to receive or able to grasp; I am the example and proof of a journey of possibility. This unfolded increasingly, with tears of joy pouring over and embracing all of me.

In all this awakening, my voice had a certain resolve: I am love.

As I moved and breathed, expressing myself through both body and mind, I declared my intention: to live and speak from love. This surrender, this commitment to love in all its forms, filled me with a sense of humble power. It was a power born from vulnerability and authenticity, from a willingness to embrace everything that love encompasses. I entrusted this fierce truth that everyone needs a love of self-acceptance. This journey of self-awareness is not just mine but a path everyone can embark on, inspiring and motivating each other along the way.

An exquisite cathartic dance began between my vulnerability and strength, permitting an unveiling of the long-suppressed need to live in love. With my higher self-guiding, I fully embrace all my beauty, love, and soul understanding through the woman I am meant to be. I now know this is what my human presence signed up for. I know this is what every individual signed up for their soul-loving contract.

My Breath of Gold dances, which I have now grown to describe, have each led me to feel and grasp all of myself. I became freer through each allowance, releasing openings of entrances and soul tunnels. I am more unshackled and can feel deeper, wonderfully allowing me to be intrigued by my wholeness. This clarity has given me insights into being a more inspiring mom, allowing me to embrace my essence through new connections, more tailored ideas for my clients, and appreciating all possibilities for myself and the world.

Each breathwork journey is a unique invitation to delve into a pure sense of self-power and soul acceptance. This empowering voyage is taken with your hands, heart, and breath. You are the sole influencer; you are in control. The ultimate act of free will is to release your soul from the old and embrace the new. Dancing with Breath of Gold is empowering because it is at your tempo and beat, in your chosen time and space, a soul-centred devotion to uncovering all you need to know to embrace, nurture, and heal yourself.

Living in an alive state is living with a whole sense of existence where you connect and appreciate yourself on every level, from how your mind works, speaks and thinks, how you stay centred, how your body physically plays, heals, and powerfully holds, and a true knowing of your oneness all to feel self-assured. All this is a genuine relationship and devotion to self, allowing a raw, honest soul-living connection that shifts the world powerfully. Behold this beauty and love coherence, and choose to value and understand the importance of self-love, self-acceptance, and the unique entwining of your golden threads.

Take this truest dance of the soul with the most essential, eloquently aligned leader.

YOU!

Adrienne Rivera

Leading Breathwork with Alive Angels

November 23, 2024

"I've never seen dad so devastated. He wasn't even like this when his mom and dad passed away."

This was the text message I received from my sister. I had no idea what she was talking about.

I was worried. My heart began to sink.

I had no idea what she was talking about.

I called her right away to see what had happened.

"Charlie suddenly passed away," my sister said.

My heart sunk. My cousin in Puerto Rico? He was so young. My sister shared with me that he passed unexpectedly while in the hospital with health issues. He had been working towards his dream of opening a barber shop for over a year. He and his dad nearly finished everything—replacing the windows, buying the chairs, and painting the walls. The grand opening was only about a month away.

I was in disbelief. A picture of Charlie flashed into my mind and I quickly pulled up his Facebook profile on my phone. As soon as I saw a picture of his face, I could see a movie in my mind of him smiling and dancing with his baby at my wedding in Puerto Rico.

Scrolling down, I saw a beautiful and touching photo of Charlie at his wedding just five years ago. A tightness rose in my chest as I burst into tears, seeing my abuela standing strong and proud beside him. And then my eyes moved to the left, to my dad. He was standing there smiling—wearing his Air Force uniform to show his respect and admiration for Charlie.

I hadn't expected to become so emotional so fast. I ended the call with my sister and immediately dialed my dad.

My mom answered.

"Dad can't really talk right now. I've never seen him like this. He's going to go to bed now. Try calling back in the morning."

When someone passes away, it often brings up layers of unresolved grief for other loved ones that have already passed. I thought about my grandparents: Oma, Abuela, and Abuelo. My grandparents were all so loving and special. The sadness of not having them alive washed over me again.

When I called Dad the next day, his voice sounded a little stronger. He told me he'd managed to get some sleep. I told him that I wanted to go to the funeral, but that I was worried I'd be a burden. What if I am a distraction? What if I just make things harder for everyone? I wrestled with these thoughts, unsure of how to navigate my own sadness while supporting my family.

He said that I didn't have to go and that no one was expecting me to. He knew how busy I was and thought that going would inconvenience me.

Despite this, I kept feeling like I had to be there. I couldn't miss this opportunity. Every other summer growing up, I'd spend weeks in Puerto Rico with my cousins, swimming in the ocean and playing in the pool. Those are some of my most cherished memories. I wanted to be there for my family now, to offer comfort and share their grief. Charlie's passing had driven home the fragility of life; I couldn't bear the thought of missing a chance to say goodbye and celebrate his life with my family.

A few days later, I found out that the funeral was happening in two days. I followed my intuition and booked a next-day flight to Puerto Rico.

November 26th, 2024

As soon as my flight landed in San Juan, Puerto Rico, I took an Uber directly to the funeral service. I showed up with my white travel backpack and black outfit. I scanned the room for family faces and then saw my mom and dad seated.

I sat beside them. I couldn't understand much of what was being said with my imperfect Spanish, but the energy was palpable. The air thick with grief, punctuated by sobs from friends and family.

Tears streamed down my face, my chest aching with each sob. I saw my family devastated, their grief echoing through the room in a chorus of sobs. I felt the weight of their love, a love that even this profound loss couldn't diminish.

At the end of the service, my mom said, *"Hey, look! That's Abuelo's sister!"*

I hadn't met her before, but she looked just like him. And she looked incredible! Her posture was perfect, her singing voice beautiful, and her smile lit up the room.

Tears flowed as I met and hugged her for the first time. It felt like Abuelo had come back to life, and I was able to hug him again. I never thought I'd feel that close to him again.

The service opened the door to deep and vulnerable conversations. My parents and I had never before talked so openly about our emotions.

Growing up, I remember conversations revolving around achievements—like my Daughters of the American Revolution Award or my sister's acceptance to William & Mary.

I have no memories from my childhood of my family openly discussing their emotions. This trip deepened our connection, allowing us to process our emotions and be authentic with one another.

Each night in Puerto Rico, we prayed the rosary as a family. It brought me closer to my abuelos (grandparents), knowing they did it every night.

This was a different type of trip–it was very healing and spiritual. And what was so beautiful was that it was healing together as a family.

It reminded me that we don't have to grieve alone.

I could feel the deep layers of grief within my relatives who all had very deep relationships with my cousin, Charlie.

I wanted to support them in a more meaningful way. Knowing breathwork could help, I offered them that healing experience.

And they all wanted to try it!

December 1, 2024

I sat in the room of my Airbnb scrambling. My relatives said YES to doing a breathwork session with me!

And they were coming over within an hour..........

I started researching AI platforms that could potentially translate one of my breathwork recordings into Spanish since I knew that many of my relatives didn't understand English.

Every resource had a ten-minute limit. I started transcribing some of my scripts into Spanish, but the words felt overwhelming. There was no way I could become fluent in an hour. I decided to surrender and trust that I was already prepared to lead the perfect session.

They showed up smiling and ready to receive with their mats and blankets. I definitely didn't feel prepared or ready.

"If only I could take a few more spanish lessons, find a printer, and print out a script to hold..." I thought to myself.

Then, the phrase I always shared with my clients came to mind:

"Everything you need lies within your breathe."

I had to trust that I already had everything I needed in that moment.

Knowing how much more meaningful breathwork experiences can be with *"space holders"*—people who offer present and hands-on support—I asked my mom if she'd be willing to help. As a former nurse with a naturally loving spirit, I knew she'd be perfect.

She felt honored and readily agreed. My dad was there as well, ready to support his family. I gave my parents a quick crash course in supportive touch during breathwork, connecting with her intuition, and energy protection.

Just as the sun began to set, we headed to the beach for the breathwork session. There I was, walking with my mom and dad on the same sand where I'd spent countless summers growing up.

This was the same beach where my mom had walked with me as a baby, where I'd visited with my family nearly every summer, and where I'd gotten married at twenty-eight.

My dad looked at me, touched his heart, and said, 'Corazón' (heart). I was honored that he trusted me to lead our family in breathwork during this challenging time of grief.

I surrendered and offered my pre-breathwork talk, using all the Spanish I knew. I released the need for perfect grammar and surprised myself with how much flowed through me.

I guided everyone to hold hands and feel Charlie's presence, to connect with nature as the waves crashed and the wind swirled around us.

Leading breathwork requires skill, confidence, education, presence, heart connection, intuition, spiritual connection, and above all, surrender to the moment.

As everyone lay in a circle with their heads toward the center, I stood in the middle and began guiding them with the words that flowed through me—a beautiful mix of 90% Spanish and 10% Spanglish.

I cleansed my energy using one of the visualization techniques I teach my students and began.

I danced between speaking and offering supportive touch to my cousins and aunts. My mom joined in, providing touch, and we communicated with our eyes. I silently reassured her, guiding her with subtle glances.

She was deeply connected to her heart; I could feel the profound wave of emotions flowing within her.

My dad stood there, deeply moved by the power of the breathwork session and the emotions it was already bringing up in our relatives in just the first 5 minutes. He then stepped in to place his hands on his sister's shoulders in a grounding and supportive way. It was so beautiful to see.

There I was, leading breathwork for my Puerto Rican family—the very people I dedicated this book to. And not only that, but alongside my mom and dad as my supporting angels!

Often, when I lead breathwork, I call in the energy of my abuela and abuelo to help protect the space and move the energy. I frequently feel their presence on a spiritual level.

Standing with my feet firmly planted in the grass at the edge of the beach, hands raised, I could sense my abuelo behind me on my left side and my abuela behind me on my right.

As I stood there, fully present, holding the space, I saw my mom and dad with their loving and supportive touch allowing people to feel so safe and supported.

It was a powerful experience, seeing my parents alive and supporting me in this way, knowing that one day, when they go to heaven, I'll call on them as angels, just like I do with Abuela and Abuelo.

It was so unique and sacred to have that experience with them. There was a deep spiritual connection that was created within all of us throughout the journey.

The experience was life-changing and profoundly healing for everyone. My aunt felt fifty pounds lighter by the end. One cousin realized she no longer wanted to be the same person she was before. Another processed unresolved emotions around her father. Another cousin felt the profound presence and love of our grandparents. Charlie's mom received confirmation that he was at peace. Nearly everyone who participated felt Charlie's spirit with them.

They felt a sense of peace, knowing they could connect with Charlie spiritually anytime through their breath.

Now, I too can call on Charlie's spirit to support me as one of my angels when I guide breathwork.

Facilitating that session was a true gift. My parents were forever changed, honored to be part of such a beautiful healing process.

Conclusion

This book could be a thousand pages long if it included every powerful testimony, every spiritual awakening sparked by breathwork. I've witnessed people heal from deep grief and childhood trauma, release deep-seated pain, and tap into a wellspring of joy they never knew existed—all through the power of conscious breathing. And this is just the beginning.

More and more people are embracing breathwork, not only for personal healing but also to become certified facilitators, sharing this transformative practice with the world.

We are stepping out of the shadows and into the light. We are embracing authenticity, vulnerability, and the full spectrum of human emotion. This is the power of breathwork—to heal, to connect, and to truly live our lives.

My story with breathwork doesn't end here. The opportunity to guide my family in a healing breathwork journey feels like a beautiful full-circle moment, one I cherish as I close this chapter of rediscovering myself and my voice.

But as we all know, the only thing constant in life is change. And with every change, every unexpected twist and turn, I am grateful to know that my breath will always be with me. Breathwork has taught me to surrender to the unknown with an open heart. Regular breathwork improves our lives, helping us release past hurts and limiting beliefs that keep us from being fully present and loving. As you've seen in these stories, it supports us in forgiveness, rewriting old narratives, and healing from within.

And it is a practice! It's a practice! We are all human. We will inevitably veer away from unconditional love at times. But when we choose to return to our breath, we can guide ourselves back on track.

It inspires me to know that many of you reading this have already said yes to becoming certified breathwork facilitators or feel the call to do so.

It is a practice! We are all human. We will inevitably veer away from unconditional love at times. But when we choose to return to our breath, we can gently guide ourselves back on track.

It inspires me to know that many of you reading this have already said yes to becoming certified breathwork facilitators or feel the call to do so.

We cannot do this alone. We need you—the healed, present, heart-centered version of you—to share this transformative practice with the world.

So, as always, remember: *"everything you need lies within your breath."*

The Adventure Begins

I want to give a big thanks to all of the authors who contributed to this book. Thank you for your openness and vulnerability. I know your stories have touched countless lives.

Many of you are graduates of the Breath of Gold Facilitator Program, have experienced breathwork with me for years, or have joined us on a retreat—perhaps even all three!

If you feel inspired to connect with any of these amazing authors, please reach out. You'll find their bios and websites at the end of this book.

And if you're feeling called to become a certified breathwork facilitator yourself, I invite you to apply for the Breath of Gold Breathwork Facilitator Program:

www.breathofgold.com/breathwork-certification-waitlist

Scan the QR code to Sign Up

If you're wanting to experience breathwork for yourself, I invite you to join us for a free breathwork journey at www.breathofgold.com/sunday-breathwork.

Scan the QR code to Apply

Author Bios

Adrienne Rivera

Adrienne Rivera is an entrepreneur, author, and breathwork facilitator with a passion for helping others create lives full of purpose and abundance. She's the heart and soul behind Breath of Gold, one of the world's fastest growing breathwork facilitator programs.

Adrienne is passionate about helping her facilitator students master their craft by incorporating powerful speaking, intuitive music selection, and deep connection to their intuition.

When she's not working with her facilitation students or leading transformative breathwork sessions, you can find Adrienne enjoying the natural beauty of Reno, Nevada, with her husband, Darren, and dog, Pike. Adrienne is a sought-after speaker and expert, who has shared her wisdom about breathwork on the TEDx stage, countless podcasts, and numerous online summits. Adrienne's creative passions shine through in her unique creations: "The Breath of Gold Oracle Deck," "The Breath of Gold" book, and "The Breath of Gold Journal" – practical tools that help individuals dive deeper into their breathwork practice.

Website

https://www.breathofgold.com/

Jeremy Youst

Jeremy Youst is a dedicated breathwork practitioner and educator with decades of experience guiding individuals on profound transformational journeys. His passion for breathwork ignited in the late 1980s after experiencing its power to unlock and integrate deep-seated emotions and beliefs stemming from childhood trauma. These early experiences led him to extensive training in various breathwork modalities, culminating in the creation of the Power of Breath Institute and Somatic Breath Therapy. Jeremy's commitment to the field extends to his contributions to the Global Professional Breathwork Alliance and the International Breathwork Federation, where he has played key roles in establishing training standards and promoting breathwork's therapeutic potential.

Driven by a deep sense of purpose, Jeremy has facilitated over 8,000 breathwork sessions, conducted numerous workshops, and led practitioner trainings in the US and Ireland. He continually refines his approach by integrating knowledge from leading trauma experts like Dr. Dan Siegel, Dr. Bessel Van der Kolk, and Dr. Stephen Porges. Jeremy's extensive experience, combined with his intuitive understanding of the "Spirit of Breath," allows him to provide highly effective and supportive guidance to those seeking deep healing and personal transformation through breathwork.

Website

https://powerofbreath.com/

Susan Peters

Susan Peters is the author of the best selling book, "The Miracle of Marrying My Heart: A Journey of Discovering New Dreams After Loss," a co-author of the international best selling book, "Manifesting Magical Moments," a speaker at "Breath of Gold Live," the creator of the "Heart to Heart Connections" Summit, creator and facilitator of "The Dreams After Loss" book reflection group, and a grief mentor.

After the unexpected and devastating loss of her beloved husband, John, she began a transformational journey of her heart to move through her grief. She discovered how creating new dreams for herself as well as learning how to connect with her own breath through Adrienne Rivera's Breath of Gold Membership helped bring her heart back into wholeness and authentic connection, allowing her to embrace the fullness of life. She hopes to inspire others to reconnect with their deepest selves after times of loss so they can learn how to dream and find the magic in their lives once again. She is in love with the life she has chosen and truly believes that connecting more with our hearts and with each other will transform the world.

Website

www.susan-peters.com

Shawn LaFountain

Shawn LaFountain is a long time music lover and classically trained percussionist. After being diagnosed with brain cancer in 2022, he embarked on a spiritual journey that led him to explore numerous healing modalities. Having a background in music, he fell in love with sound healing as a modality to thrive through his cancer healing journey. In addition to being certified as an expert sound healing facilitator, he is also a Breath of Gold certified breathwork facilitator and reiki master. Shawn lives in Austin, TX with his eight year old son and enjoys hiking and paddleboarding in his spare time.

Website

https://soulstreamhealing.com

Tracey-Ann Rose

Ever since Tracey-Ann Rose was a little girl in Tennessee, she knew she wanted to stand out and make a real difference. Tracey-Ann bounced between career paths - from acting to writing, but she finally felt at home when she discovered energy healing.

She started out by offering beta sessions to friends, family members, and eventually a BIPOC Manifestation group - and it blew up. Tracey-Ann was booked out for a month and a half and finally started charging for her work.

In her sessions, she didn't just talk to her beta clients about healing, but about thriving. By leveraging their unique energy, she discovered what made each woman unique and how her clients could leverage their gifts in their professional and personal life.

The transformations were phenomenal. Not only did these women start to see themselves differently, but they also started to live differently, more aligned with who they truly were. After Tracey-Ann concluded the sessions, she did a follow-up survey. One hundred percent of the women experienced deeper clarity, and the majority of which also drastically changed their careers.

That's why she became a Certified Spiritual Sales Coach. She wanted to create a space for WOC to build up a healthy mindset, have work-life balance, and create their business as she had - guided by her strengths, passions and purpose.

Website
https://www.traceyannrose.com/

Erin Cummings

Erin Cummings is a writer and advocate for self-healing, who bravely shares her personal experiences with body image, self-acceptance, and the impact of childhood trauma. In her contributing chapter to the Breath of Gold Book, "In Which She Learns the Word 'Conviviality'," she shares her experiences with breathwork, revealing its profound impact on her journey toward healing and wholeness. She writes about powerful breathwork journeys where she confronts limiting beliefs about her appearance, connects with ancestral energies, and receives channeled messages from her spirit guides. She explores the challenges of overcoming insecurities, embracing her authentic self, and releasing the need for external validation. Her story is a testament to the power of breathwork to facilitate deep emotional release and self-discovery.

In Erin's every day live, she works as a teacher. In her spare time, she loves using her funny and quirky personality to do improv comedy where she lives in Reno, Nevada. She is a big foodie–and loves cooking amazing recipes that all of her friends love. She is also a certified Breath of Gold Breathwork Facilitator.

Website:

https://www.instagram.com/erinkathleencummings/

Rachel Gossett

Rachel is a graduate of the Breath of Gold Breathwork Facilitator Program and a co-author of the Breath of Gold book. Rachel works full-time as a speech-language pathologist in New Jersey, where she supports the special-needs community. Additionally, she serves as a Reiki Master, Breathwork Facilitator, and hospice volunteer.

She is passionate about sharing her story about her healing journey and wants to spread the message that healing IS possible! In her coaching and breathwork business, specializes in working with people who struggle with their relationship with food and their bodies to achieve "food freedom." She believes that her freedom starts from within and healing from our past.

Website

https://reikibyrae.com

Terese-Weinstein Katz

Terese Weinstein Katz, MFT, PhD, is a licensed psychologist with a long and active career dedicated to helping individuals navigate life's challenges and unlock their full potential. Her journey with breathwork began as a powerful rediscovery during a period of intense personal change and loss. She recognized its profound ability to connect individuals to their core emotions and needs, often revealing those hidden beneath the surface. Dr. Katz embraces a holistic approach to well-being, acknowledging the value of various support systems, including therapy, friendships, exercise, and bodywork. However, she views breathwork as a unique pathway for releasing deeply held tensions stemming from trauma or anxiety. She is particularly drawn to its ability to foster creativity and insight, bypassing the limitations of the conscious mind.

As a facilitator, Dr. Katz guides individuals and small groups through breathwork experiences, emphasizing the importance of a safe and supportive environment. She believes in creating a "set and setting" conducive to transformative journeys, akin to the concept of "psychedelic experiences without drugs" as described by Dr. Richard Shaub. Dr. Katz's approach is trauma-informed, ensuring participants feel secure as they explore their inner landscape. She acts as a guide and coach, helping individuals integrate the insights and releases that emerge during their breathwork sessions. Dr. Katz is passionate about empowering individuals to experience not only emotional release and newfound awareness, but also lasting perspective shifts that can positively impact their lives.

Website

https://sapphirebreathwork.com/

Kara Stoltenberg

Kara Stoltenberg, MA, Ed., empowers individuals to break free from limiting narratives and embrace lives of authenticity and purpose. Through online communities, live events, and individual coaching, she provides a safe and supportive space for transformative change.
Drawing from her own journey of overcoming adversity and rediscovering self-love, Kara guides clients to implement simple yet powerful practices that foster balance in mind, body, and spirit. She helps individuals honor their past experiences without being defined by them, empowering you to write the story you want to live rather than being limited by the narratives of your past.

As an international best-selling author, teacher, and spiritual guide, Kara combines genuine care with intuitive mentorship. She facilitates the release of blocked emotions and beliefs, empowering clients to achieve their personal and health goals. Her compassionate approach fosters a deep sense of safety and trust, allowing individuals to fully embrace their healing journey and step into their full potential.

Website

https://www.karastoltenberg.com/

Simona Luna

Simona Luna is a Spiritual Business Coach, Inspirational Speaker and Host of The Moon Tribe podcast. She helps conscious entrepreneurs grow their business with alignment and flow so they can live their full potential.

In her late thirties, she decided to leave her career in the creative industry behind to follow her true purpose as a spiritual mentor. An entrepreneur since 2011, she has been guiding her clients over the last 5 years to create dream businesses while elevating their lives to the next level.

Simona has been featured on the cover of Yoga Magazine and is a regular speaker at international events.

Born in Vienna, her free spirit has taken her to live in London, Helsinki, Melbourne and Amsterdam. Nowadays, she's enjoying life in the countryside in Portugal with her partner.

Website

https://www.simonaluna.com

Amy Quinn

Amy Quinn is an advocate for health and wellness. She weats many hats as a coach, school teacher, tour guide, and fitness instructor. She is also a certified Breath of Gold Breathwork Facilitator. She has used breathwork as a powerful tool to change her life, which she shares about in her contributing chapter in the Breath of Gold Book, "Freeing Myself from an Addictive Lover." She is the mama of three gorgeous kids and her doodle, Joy. She lives in the Applachain Mountains.

Website

https://www.instagram.com/amyquinn8067/

Veronica Galipo

Veronica Galipo is a transformative Self-Love and Life Coach, Hypnotherapist Practitioner, and author dedicated to empowering individuals to "build their souls to their strongest state of being, so they can rise and ripple their essence to the world."

Since 2018, Veronica has guided profound personal transformations through an integrative approach rooted in ancestral wisdom, spiritual awareness, and neurological insights. Her rich heritage—blending Australian roots with her passionate Latin lineage—infuses her work with a deeply human and authentic perspective.

Believing that "Embracing yourself fully, free of judgment, is the most radical act of self-love," Veronica helps individuals break free from limiting narratives, reconnect with their authentic selves, and rewrite their stories. Her unique framework combines neuroscience, intuitive techniques, and self-love practices to guide others in reclaiming their inherent worth and strength.

Having overcome the weight of cultural expectations and self-doubt, Veronica now leads others on bold journeys of self-discovery, helping them heal, grow, and align with their truth. She inspires resilience, clarity, and meaningful transformation through coaching, workshops, books, and heartfelt interviews.

Veronica's mission is to create a ripple of change, one soul at a time, by helping individuals unlock their potential through the power of self-love and authentic living.

Website

https://veronicagalipo.com.au/

Let the Journey Continue

Apply for the Breath of Gold Breathwork Facilitator Program

Scan the QR code to Sign Up

Try for a Free Breath of Gold Breathwork Session

Scan the QR code to Apply

Made in the USA
Monee, IL
01 January 2025

75721321R00085